Boxing PLATO'S SHADOW

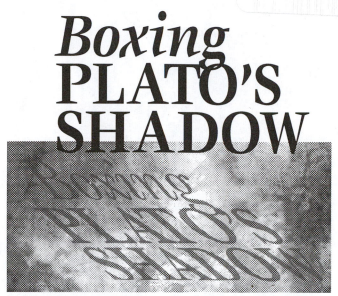

The Study of Human Communication

Michael Dues
Mary Brown

University of Arizona

The McGraw-Hill Companies, Inc.
Primis Custom Publishing

*New York St. Louis San Francisco Auckland Bogotá
Caracas Lisbon London Madrid Mexico Milan Montreal
New Delhi Paris San Juan Singapore Sydney Tokyo Toronto*

McGraw·Hill

A Division of The McGraw·Hill Companies

Boxing Plato's Shadow
The Study of Human Communication

McGraw-Hill's Primis Custom Publishing consists of products that are produced from camera-ready copy. Peer review, class testing, and accuracy are primarily the responsibility of the author(s).

1 2 3 4 5 6 7 8 9 0   BKM BKM   9 0 9 8
ISBN 0-07-039675-2

Editor: Julie Kehrwald
Cover Design: Maggie Lytle
Printer/Binder: Book-Mart Press, Inc.

Contents

Foreword

This book is about *the systematic study of communication*, and about efforts to apply the knowledge produced by this study to achieve better outcomes. Anyone who seeks to become a professional scholar, teacher, or practitioner of communication should have a basic understanding of the origins of our ideas about communication, the key issues with which communication scholars struggle, and the processes by which knowledge about communication is generated. We hope in this small volume to provide a starting point for this understanding by presenting the rhetorical and social scientific roots of communication study.

M.D. and M.B.

Introduction
Communication Study: A Discipline of Refugees

Robert Gunderson, a venerable communication scholar and teacher, once described Communication Study as a discipline of refugees. He observed that most communication scholars began their academic careers intending to be something else—to be psychologists, sociologists, or historians. "We came to this study as refugees," he said, "because there were important questions to answer about communication that we couldn't address adequately in our home disciplines." Dr. Gunderson was talking about professional scholars more than twenty years ago, but the same phenomenon seems to occur today when college students choose their major. Very few of our students came to the university intending to major in Communication; most came to the discipline as refugees when they discovered that by studying communication they could gain interesting and useful knowledge and skills which they could not acquire in their original majors.

One reason people do not initially focus on becoming communication scholars is that they are simply not aware that a discrete discipline of communication study exists. And, if they are aware that it exists, they have only the vaguest ideas about what communication scholars study. A second reason is that in our American culture communication tends to be viewed only as a process, as if there were no connection between what we say and how we say it. We tend to believe that *action* really counts, while *talk* is "just talk." Thus, communication is not seen as central or important until it fails. If communication as a profession has either no image at all, or a negative image as a non-substantial, flim-flam occupation, one can expect as a communication student, scholar, or professional practitioner, to be often overlooked, often misunderstood, and occasionally suspect. Communication professionals regularly confront the necessity to explain themselves, their discipline, and their profession.

I (Michael Dues) first encountered this necessity when, after completing an MA in American History, and teaching history for several years, I chose to pursue my doctorate in Communication. My former major professor in History made it clear that he was genuinely disappointed in me. "I think that's a serious mistake," he said. "If you're serious about your academic career you'll need your doctorate in an established discipline, like history, or psychology. Speech Communication just isn't a substantial academic discipline." He was wrong, of course, but his view was, and still is, a common one. A college dean at a major university, for example, recently suggested that she could not imagine a university without a psychology or sociology department, but she *could easily* imagine a university without a communication department. Outside the university, in my consulting work, clients usually assume that my doctorate is either in psychology or in business. When I tell them my degree is in communication, they are surprised, even though I am identified as a communication specialist. When I ask why they are surprised, they usually say "I didn't know you could get a Ph.D. in Communication."

Most high school students, and many high school counselors, are still unaware that one can major in communication in college. Assessments designed to help students choose potential careers do not have a career category for communication other than public relations or mass media. So there is very little reason why one should come to college intending to major in the study of communication. Moreover, when one becomes a communication major, one typically faces misguided questions from parents and other relatives like, "*Communications*? Do you mean TV broadcasting?" Or "Communication? What can you do with *that*?" Communication is often wrongly viewed as a "soft" or "easy" major. So, even as undergraduates, communication majors confront the task of explaining or defending their discipline.

Given the widespread ignorance about the study of communication in contemporary society, it is understandable that scholars, professionals, and students come to the discipline as refugees. Yet, once engaged, we quickly see that communication is central to human interaction, that greater skill in communication means greater ability to meet our own, our family's, and our community's needs, and that improved communication can mean improved quality of life.

Why is the study of human communication so undervalued in the twentieth century? Why do we encounter these troubling paradoxes in which so central and important a subject is so little recognized in the academy, and in which the ability to influence millions with words may be less honored than ability to move a few by force? These are puzzling paradoxes and troublesome questions which we try to answer in the chapters that follow.

Chapter I
The Beginning of Communication
Study and Plato's Dark Shadow

To appreciate the study of human communication, and to answer our questions about its puzzling paradoxes, we must know
its history. And we must begin at the beginning of the story, in
ancient Athens.

During the fifth century BC, Athens reached the peak of its
economic and military prominence. Arguably the strongest and
wealthiest of Greek city states, Athens had merchant ships trading
throughout the Mediterranean basin, a great navy, a powerful army,
magnificent structures and beautiful art. The great Athenian legacy
that concerns us here, however, resulted not from the city's power
or its beauty, but from two important innovations in its governance:
the adversary system of justice, and democracy.

The Adversary System was invented by the Greeks as an alternative to fighting among themselves. The basic premise of this
system was that when two citizens found themselves in a dispute
over property or some perceived offense, they would agree in advance to let a respected third party serve as judge. Each of the
disputing parties would argue his case before the judge who, based
upon his evaluation of the merits of their arguments, would decide
how the dispute should be settled. In settling conflicts among

citizens, this approach amounted to replacing physical combat with verbal combat, which was an obvious improvement. Over time this approach was formalized into a court system, and was extended to apply to judging the guilt or innocence of persons accused of crimes. Although, in subsequent centuries various states have added and improved details, the adversary system remains the best available judicial process.

Democracy was adopted as a replacement for tyranny in Athens during the sixth century BC. Tyranny is the form of governance in which a single ruler has absolute, unquestioned authority over everything. With a wise and beneficent ruler tyranny can be tolerable; with a bad tyrant it is extremely oppressive. So, under the innovative leadership of Solon and Cleisthenes, Athens instituted reforms, adopting a system of government in which citizens assembled and made decisions by majority vote. Thereafter, the Athenian Assembly debated and decided by voting on such matters as official appointments, laws, declaring war, or accepting a proposed peace treaty. This was democracy in an embryonic form. Only a small minority of the Athenian population—male citizens—participated. Women were forbidden to speak publicly, or to vote. Non-citizen merchants, traders, professionals, and ambassadors were excluded, as were slaves. Still, the ancient Athenians invented, and successfully applied, the basic method of democratic governance.

A Market for Communication Knowledge and Skill

In Athenian courts citizens were required to advocate cases for themselves; and citizens spoke for themselves in the Assembly. The ability to speak persuasively was thus a skill one needed to function as an Athenian citizen. Moreover, people who were more skilled in speaking than others had an obvious advantage. They won court cases and thus acquired more wealth; they also acquired position, status, and power by being impressive and influential in the Assembly. Success in public speaking became a means to greater wealth, status, and power. As Athenian citizens sought to improve their speaking ability, they created an obvious market for knowledge and skills in public speaking. Since these skills had monetary and status value, Athenians were willing to pay for them.

The Sophists

The systematic study of communication began in Athens during the 5th century BC in response to this market. Persons who studied and taught persuasive public speaking were known as *sophists*. They called this subject *rhetoric*. Most sophists charged fees for their services; they were professional teachers.

The term "sophist" had been used in Athens since the sixth century BC to refer to learned men, wise men, poets, and teachers (Barrett, 1987, p. 3). The most important and influential of the early sophists were foreigners in Athens, ambassadors or traveling teachers from other cities. Each taught a broad range of subjects in addition to rhetoric; each taught that one needed to be broadly learned and wise in order to be a truly good speaker. Harold Barrett tells us they offered a curriculum "designed to teach the Greek ideal of *arete:* the knowledge and attitude of effective participation in domestic, social, and political life" (1987, p. 5). Sophists believed that all reasonably intelligent persons could become knowledgeable and acquire the skills to speak well—a view that offended some older, more traditional and elitist Athenians who clung to the belief that one's destiny was predetermined at birth.

Some of the sophists contributed important insights into communication and social interaction that have endured, and which still influence the study and practice of communication. Below are six examples.

Protagoras, who was probably the first person to charge a fee for teaching, contributed the important idea that there are two sides to every argument. Protagoras suggested that the "truth" of one side should be tested by the "truth" of the other, and that advocates for each side have the burden of proving their side stronger (Barrett, 1987, p. 10).

Gorgias was noted for his beautiful style in the use of language. He focused on oratory that bordered on poetry, and he taught that through great oratory one could "stop fear and banish grief and create joy and nurture piety" (Barrett, 1987, p. 15). Gorgias also appears to have developed the concept of *kairos*, which states that a speaker should adapt his oratory to suit the audience and the occasion (Barrett, 1987, p. 19).

Prodicus was noted for emphasizing the importance of precision in the use of language and of recognizing subtleties and nuances. He brought rigor, discipline, and attention to detail to the study of rhetoric (Barrett, 1987, p 18).

Thrasymachus contributed the important idea of a "middle style" in speaking, a style in between the grand oratory of Gorgias and plain talk (Barrett, 1987, p. 23). The concept of different speaking styles for different occasions and conditions built upon Gorgias' idea of *kairos.*

Hippias advocated that speakers must be broadly knowledgeable, able to answer all questions about a subject. He taught that it was necessary to keep acquiring new knowledge throughout one's life. This teaching led to a famous debate with Socrates, in which Hippias argued that it was important to always have new things to say on a subject, while Socrates countered that truth was eternal, and that it was more important to speak the same enduring truths consistently (Barrett, 1987, p. 22).

Isocrates (who married the daughter of Hippias) worked and taught in the 4th century BC, and apparently brought together much of the teaching of fifth century sophists in a written handbook. All copies of Isocrates' handbook were apparently destroyed, but later important writers on rhetoric, including Aristotle, Cicero, and

Quintillian clearly drew much from it in developing their own thought (Kennedy, 1963, pp. 71-73).

Taken together, the sophists not only began the systematic study of communication, but also brought about major advances in Greek thought. They challenged the older Athenian beliefs that humans were at the mercy of existing natural laws, and that human lives were predetermined re-enactments of archetypal events that had already occurred among the gods. They advocated the revolutionary idea that humans are social creatures who can affect their own environment and their personal and community fortunes, and who can influence one another by communicating effectively. They proposed that truth could be effectively pursued by testing ideas in debate. They advanced the profoundly democratic idea that *everyone* can *and should* learn to speak well and become influential (Barrett, 1987, pp. 36-37). And they taught that developing the skills and knowledge needed for citizenship was the duty of each citizen. The fundamental concepts and skills provided by the sophists made democracy possible. The practical study of "rhetoric" which they developed became a central subject in education curricula, and remained so for more than 1,000 years.

Given the important contributions made by the sophists to the development of Greek thought, to Western Civilization, and to the study of human communication, it seems oddly paradoxical that they and their subject are held today in such low esteem. This paradox is at least somewhat understandable when we consider two factors:

1. There is a dark side to studying and developing skill in communication; communication is the favorite tool of con artists and demagogues.
2. Plato wrote so eloquently in arguing against the sophists' point of view that he cast a seemingly permanent dark shadow across the sophists and their work.

The Dark Side of Communication

Communication itself is neither good nor bad (Burgoon, Hunsaker & Dawson, 1994). It is a tool that can be used as readily to deceive as to inform. In every era of history, there have been con artists who deceive and manipulate others through communication. Con artists and demagogues make a point of becoming effective persuaders, using every known rhetorical device to achieve their ends. For them effective communication is successful trickery. So, for many people, being persuaded becomes associated with being fooled, mislead, deceived, or defrauded. Some later sophists were less ethical than those we discussed above. Some went so far as to claim that truth did not matter, only effective persuasive technique. The reputations of the sophists, and of the study of rhetoric suffered accordingly.

Plato's Dark Shadow

During the fifth century BC, military and economic success changed Athens from a close-knit city state whose citizens shared coherent beliefs and values, into a cosmopolitan metropolis populated by diverse people who spoke different languages, held varying beliefs, and practiced a variety of customs. Foreigners brought to Athens attractive new ideas and goods, many of which challenged old Athenian ideas and customs. Many Athenians viewed these changes as corruptions of their pure beliefs and values; they longed for, and advocated returning to, Athens' older, purer values and simpler ways (Barrett, 1987, p. 28). When Athens began to lose battles and wealth during the 4th century BC, these conservatives attributed their city's decline to its straying from traditional values under the influence of foreigners. Sophists who offered new ideas were controversial in Athens because they were seen by many as subverting traditional Athenian beliefs (Barrett, 1987, p. 28).

In Athens Socrates was an important and, to some, troubling voice. He challenged not traditional Athenian beliefs, but the newer ideas and mores associated with democratic governance that had taken hold in the fifth century BC (Smith, 1998, pp. 56-61). Uncomfortable with governance by a majority of ordinary men who were not particularly learned or wise, he sought to limit movement toward expanded democracy. He was suspicious of attempts by people to persuade one another, which formed the basis of the new democratic process. Believing that humans are to seek Truth by going inside themselves, he sought to help individuals discover truth not by persuading them, but only by asking questions during dialogues. Socrates rarely made speeches or presented arguments; rather, he professed to know very little, and preferred to ask challenging questions which provoked deeper thought on the part of his hearers. His method of drawing out, or "educing" truths from his students, is still applied; we call it the "Socratic method" today. And the Greek word "educe," which means to draw out, is the root of our word, "Education."

Socrates' most influential follower was Plato, the most literate and articulate conservative of his day. Plato opposed democracy on the fundamental grounds that truth is fixed and should be sought only by philosophers. The central point in his great work, *The Republic*, is that the best government would be one in which the best philosopher rules as king. Plato was uncomfortable with the idea that ordinary citizens should presume to advocate or to participate in governmental decision-making (Kennedy, 1967, pp 15-16; Smith, 1998, pp. 56-61).

Plato viewed the sophists and their ideas as harmful influences in Athens. He treated the sophists as enemies, and sought to discredit them as completely as possible. He did not distinguish between good and bad sophists; he painted them all with the same dark brush. He objected to the study of rhetoric as a discrete subject on the grounds that rhetoricians favored style over substance and valued technique more than truth. The best he could say for rhetoric was that it might be seen as a utilitarian craft, about equal to cookery in difficulty or complexity, that might be used by philosophers to explain truths to ordinary citizens (Kennedy, 1967, pp. 15-16, 162-163).

Plato presented himself as a purist in pursuit of universal Truth, and he cast Socrates in his written dialogues as the ethical inquirer in contrast to the unethical sophists (Smith, 1998, pp. 58-61). Plato's motives, however, were not entirely pure. His attacks on the sophists were self-serving, since he operated a school, charged fees for instruction, and was in direct competition with the sophists for students. It is also interesting to note that Plato used Socrates in his written dialogues as a potent *rhetorical device* to advance his persuasive arguments against rhetoric and the sophists—a strategy which enacted some of the very behaviors to which he was objecting. Nevertheless, Plato was so eloquent and potent in his attacks on rhetoric and the sophists that he succeeded in casting a permanent dark shadow over their reputations.

Aristotle's Resolution

Aristotle was Plato's student. Aristotle studied, taught, and wrote about literally every subject known to the ancient Greeks. He saw merit in both Plato's and the sophists' positions concerning the study of rhetoric, and applied himself to discovering ways to reconcile the two opposing views (Kennedy, 1991, pp. 12-13). While he respected and admired Plato, and sometimes served as an instructor in Plato's school, Aristotle differed with his great mentor on several key issues.

1. While Plato sought Truth as a philosopher, using reasoning and dialogue to "draw out" knowledge and understanding, Aristotle sought to understand his natural and social environment as a scientist would, by systematically observing.

Aristotle has been called the first true empiricist because he practiced systematic observation, using the senses, then applied logic to his observations to form conclusions about nature, and about people. For Socrates and Plato, Truth resided within the person, and was to be discovered by being drawn out. For Aristotle, Truth was all around in the environment, and was to be taken in through the senses.

2. While Plato sought only *certain* truth through philosophical thought, Aristotle observed that certainty was possible only on some matters. He noted that on many issues humans could at best ascertain "probable" truth. And he understood that most decisions in matters of state rested not on certainties but on these relative probabilities. Important decisions were made on the basis of judgments about what is probable.

3. On matters where only probable truth could be ascertained, Aristotle recognized persuasion and advocacy as valid decision making tools. He observed that persuasive advocacy in fact influenced decisions in both the courts and the Assembly. And he reasoned that, on matters where certainty could not be reached, advocacy and debate were the best available means of discovering what was most probably true.

4. Plato viewed the study and practice of rhetorical technique as promoting falsehood over truth, and thus steered honorable men away from rhetoric. Aristotle, on the other hand, saw that rhetoric could be used to promote either falsehood or truth, and he concluded that it was the *duty* of honorable citizens to arm themselves with knowledge and skill in rhetoric in order to defend truth.

5. Aristotle reasoned that truth is naturally easier to defend than falsehood. Thus, he argued, if honorable men are well armed with rhetorical skills they should always be able to prevail over the advocates of falsehood. If good men fail to develop rhetorical skill, he said, they will have only themselves to blame when falsehood prevails.

Based upon the above rationale, Aristotle studied and taught rhetoric. He drew upon many of the ideas of the sophists, added useful concepts of his own, and developed a complete system of rhetoric. Aristotle's system was laid out in his *Rhetoric*, which is recognized as the most complete of all ancient works on the subject, and which provides the starting point for most twentieth century study of persuasive communication. Aristotle defined "rhetoric" as "the art of discovering all the available means of persuasion in a given situation" (Kennedy, 1991, p. 14).

Many of the basic concepts that frame and guide our contemporary study of human communication were articulated by Aristotle in the *Rhetoric*. These include the following:

- Communication is "purposive." That is, people communicate with the *intention* of affecting or influencing others, and communication efforts can be evaluated on the basis of whether they succeeded, if so, how, and if not, why not.
- Communication efforts (oratory) can be categorized by purpose and situation into three types: *forensic oratory* is speaking in the courts as an adversary; *deliberative oratory* is speaking in the assembly to influence a decision; *epideictic* oratory is speaking at a ceremony on a special occasion to inpire listeners.
- Persuasion is accomplished through a combination of three kinds of appeals:

    Ethos (Personal appeal of the speaker. Today we call this "source credibility.")
    Logos (Logical support provided by the speaker. Today we call this argument.)
    Pathos (Emotional appeal, the stimulating of an emotional response in the audience.)

- Learning to speak effectively is a matter of developing five skills:

Invention is the ability to generate the ideas needed to be persuasive in a given situation.

Disposition is the ability to organize the ideas for maximum impact.

Style is the ability to use language appropriately in any situation.

Memory is the ability to remember facts and ideas.

Delivery is the ability to speak in a clear, strong voice and with effective gestures.

These five skill areas are commonly called Aristotle's **"five canons of rhetoric."**

During Aristotle's lifetime Athens was conquered, along with the rest of Greece, by the Macedonians. Because he was recognized as the greatest scholar and teacher in Greece, Aristotle was drafted into the service of King Philip of Macedon, and brought to his court to serve as teacher to Philip's son, Alexander. The Macedonian conquest of Greece effectively ended Athenian democracy and closed the Athenian chapter in the development of communication study.

Aristotle's *Rhetoric* survived the fall of Athens. Alexander, whom we now know as Alexander the Great, took copies of Aristotle's works along on his conquest of the then known world, and had them translated into Arabic and Persian languages. A century later, when the Romans conquered Greece, they were eager to acquire Greek knowledge. Aristotle's *Rhetoric* and the writings of the sophists served as key sources of rhetorical understanding for Cicero, Rome's greatest orator and, later, for Quintillian, who taught rhetoric in Rome (Clarke, 1953, pp. 10-15). Two thousand years later, the *Rhetoric* inspired nineteenth century English rhetoricians, George Campbell, Richard Whately, and Hugh Blair (Smith, 1998, pp. 250-263). And, in twentieth century American universities, the *Rhetoric* became the cornerstone of the academic discipline of Speech Communication.

Aristotle provided a solid foundation for the study of human communication, but his work did not dispel the doubts and suspicions about rhetoric and the sophists which Plato had raised. To this day the term "mere rhetoric" is used to refer to hollow persuasive messages, lacking substance. "Sophistry" is understood to mean specious argument, or the tricky use of style to deceive an audience. Sophists still are generally regarded as shallow thinkers and mercenaries who lacked a moral compass, in contrast to Socrates, who is viewed as the highly ethical martyr to his beliefs. Plato's negative portrayal of rhetoric and its teachers in his dialogues the *Gorgias,* and the *Phaedras* still rings true for readers. Twenty-five hundred years later, the dark shadow Plato cast over the study of persuasive communication persists.

The study of rhetoric has remained controversial partly because the ability to communicate persuasively is a potent source of power. Thus, having large numbers of people develop and apply rhetorical skills is threatening to those in power. Over the centuries, threatened individuals and institutions have often presumed to occupy Plato's high moral ground, challenged the value and ethics of rhetoric, and sought to constrict or prevent its study and practice. Two kinds of institutions that have been particularly problematic in inhibiting the study and practice of rhetoric are totalitarian governments and dogmatic religions.

Totalitarian Governments. Totalitarian governments seek to limit and restrict advocacy by anyone other than appointed spokespersons and institutions. Democracy in Athens was interrupted in 403 BC when a group of thirty citizens (including several of Plato's close relatives) who were assigned the task of drafting new democratic reforms seized power instead, suspended democratic processes, and ruled by decree for several brutal years. Among the first decrees issued by these "Thirty Tyrants," was a prohibition against the teaching of rhetoric. Free speech, unrestricted advocacy, and the teaching of effective speaking techniques thrive in open democracies, and are incompatible with tyranny. Totalitarian regimes must control thoughts and beliefs to remain in power; hence, they must control speaking and the teaching of speaking.

<u>Dogmatic</u> <u>Religions</u>. A dogmatic religion is one that promulgates a set of specific beliefs, and holds that one *must* adhere to these beliefs in order to achieve salvation. Advocacy of ideas contrary to such dogma is viewed as leading people morally astray. So, dogmatic religions tend to try to restrict any advocacy that might be contrary to their dogma, and they have often resorted with the help of government officials to brutal means in suppressing heretical advocacy. Romans imprisoned, tortured, and killed Christians to stop them from preaching that Roman gods were false and powerless. The Catholic Church had its Index of forbidden books, and its Inquisition, burning at the stake persons who advocated beliefs deemed to be heretical. Protestants were equally brutal in territories they controlled in attempting to silence "popish" preachers. In Islamic countries controlled by religious leaders today, freedom of speech is viewed as harmful, and the penalty for advocating a disapproved view can be death. Where established dogmatic religions hold sway, teaching of rhetoric is limited so that rhetoric is only studied and applied in the service of approved theology.

Boxing Plato's Shadow

Humans are highly sophisticated social animals who influence one another, coordinate activity, and achieve most of their goals through communication. By whatever name it is called, the *subject* of human communication will always be of keen interest to anyone wishing to understand human behavior, and skill in communication will always be useful and important. So, the study of communication will persist.

Because it is a potent social tool, communication will always be used by some to deceive and defraud others. A line in an old Woody Guthrie song says "Some rob you with a six gun, some with a fountain pen." In democracies, there will always be demagogues and crooked politicians who work at perfecting the art of the lie. Sharing their expertise in communication with such disreputable characters, communication practitioners and scholars will always be somewhat suspect. Moreover, given our particular cultural heritage, they will likely continue to labor under the shadow cast upon their profession by Plato.

Years ago, as a young college professor, I (Michael Dues) spent a heated hour arguing with a film instructor about the value of teaching students rhetorical sensitivity and skills. My arguments, which seemed so strong and clear to me, seemed not to move him at all. He, of course, cited Socrates and Plato, holding that truth must be "educed, which means drawn out" of students by asking challenging questions." Driving home that evening, thinking about the afternoon's discussion, it occurred to me that I had not been arguing with my contemporary colleague so much as I had been doing battle with Plato's shadow. The image came to mind of shadow boxing—skillfully swinging my fists at air, striking nothing. I felt that I had spent the afternoon boxing Plato's shadow. And, over the thirty years since that afternoon, I have learned from repeated experience that professionals in the study, teaching, or practice of communication are regularly required to address and overcome Plato's influence.

References

Barrett, H. (1987). *The Sophists.* Novato, CA: Chandler & Sharp Publishers, Inc.

Burgoon, H. M., Hunsaker, F., & Dawson, E. (1994). *Human communication.* Thousand Oaks, CA: Sage.

Clarke, M. L. (1953). *Rhetoric at Rome: A historical survey.* London, England: Cohen & West Ltd.

Kennedy, G. (1991). *Aristotle on rhetoric: A theory of civic discourse.* New York: Oxford University Press.

Kennedy, G. (1967). *The art of persuasion in Greece.* Princeton, NJ: Princeton University Press.

Smith, C. R. (1998). *Rhetoric and human consciousness: A history.* Prospect Heights, IL: Waveland Press.

Chapter 2
A Brief History of Communication Study from Aristotle to the 20th Century

In Chapter 1 we established that communication study is a 2500 year old discipline, begun in ancient Athens by the sophists, elevated to a systematic discipline by Aristotle, and effectively disparaged by Plato. We noted that present day communication scholars and professionals still labor under the shadow cast over their discipline by Plato many centuries ago. In this chapter, we briefly outline the history of the discipline from Aristotle's time to the twentieth century. We do not attempt to offer a complete or balanced history of the discipline. Rather, we try to tell the story of communication study in a way that makes clear five important points. These are:

1. The study and practice of persuasive public communication (rhetoric) has advanced and flourished in democratic times and places. Conversely, the study and practice of rhetoric has been limited and weak in autocratic times and places.
2. Ever since Plato, the study of communication has been controversial among scholars regarding its proper relationship to philosophy, theology, and science. Some insist that communica-

tion should be viewed only as a tool by which those who possess the Truth can convey it to others, while many rhetoricians assert that communication is also an appropriate means by which people can seek to discover probable truth. The question is "Can argument and debate lead us to probable truth? Or, should we presume to argue only after we have discovered Truth?"

3. The development of the study of communication has not been a steady march forward. Instead, it is a story of great advances during short periods of intellectual activity, followed by loss of interest and knowledge, followed by periods of recovery and new advances.

4. Important chapters in the history of communication study occurred outside of Europe and the United States. For fully half of its history the most important works and ideas on rhetoric resided in North Africa under the care of Egyptians and, later, Muslims. These works were returned to Spain by the Moors sometime in the eighth century, and were not recovered by Western Europeans until 1085 AD.

5. During the nineteenth and twentieth centuries communication study has expanded from its initial narrow focus on persuasive public address (rhetoric) to include a full range of communication codes, functions, and contexts.

Classical Rhetoric: Greeks, Egyptians, and Romans

Egypt

In Chapter 1 we described how the Athenians developed and matured the study of persuasive communication, culminating in Aristotle's Rhetoric. We noted that Aristotle became the teacher of Alexander the Great. Convinced of the value of the knowledge he had gained from Aristotle, Alexander took a veritable library of writings from Aristotle, Plato, the sophists, and other Greeks along when he conquered Persia and Egypt. Intending to rule his newly conquered empire from an entirely new capitol which would reflect the many cultures of all his subjects, Alexander began construction of the city of Alexandria in Egypt. Near the very center of that city he ordered construction of a great library to house all the important Greek works as well as writings from Egypt, Persia, and other newly conquered states. He ordered that all these works be translated into Arabic so that all scholars in his new empire could learn from them.

Alexander did not live to see his city or his library completed. He became ill (or perhaps he was poisoned) shortly after completing his conquests and died at the age of 33 in 323 BC. His only son, still an infant, was murdered immediately after Alexander's death and, since there was no heir to the throne, the empire was divided up. Ptolemy Soter, one of Alexander's loyal lieutenants, ruled in Alexandria and completed construction of the library as Alexander had wished (Easton, 1966, p. 82). There the works of Aristotle and the sophists were preserved in their Arabic translations and studied by Egyptian and, later, Muslim scholars. Virtually all the works of the sophists were destroyed in a fire at the Alexandria library, but many of Aristotle's works survived.

Ptolemy preserved the writings on rhetoric, but rhetoric was not a vital subject of study in Egypt under his rule. Exploiting the tradition of having a Pharaoh in Egypt, Ptolemy and his successors ruled absolutely, and tolerated no advocacy of unapproved views. Centuries later, when North Africa was under Islamic control, Muslim scholars studied the texts in the Alexandria library, but they were not particularly concerned with writings on rhetoric, since such skills were not recognized as important in their autocratic society. So, rather than advancing the study of rhetoric, Egyptian and Muslim scholars and philosophers advanced the studies of mathematics, engineering, and architecture.

Rome

While Ptolemy and his successors ruled in Egypt, Rome grew powerful and conquered the entire Mediterranean basin. Our image of Rome is that of an empire ruled absolutely by an emperor. However, during most of the period of successful Roman conquest, Rome was a republic, governed by democratic processes, with an Assembly elected by ordinary citizens (who were called "plebs"), and a Senate, representing the aristocrats (who were called "patricians"). Thus, while the subject of rhetoric was of little interest in Alexandria, it was of great interest in Rome. When Rome conquered Greece during the second century BC, Romans eagerly gathered and applied Greek knowledge and art. Soon Greek was spoken as a second language by all educated Romans. The works of Aristotle and the sophists were studied carefully. And the study and teaching of rhetoric were incorporated as central features in Roman education.

The Romans were not so much contributors of new ideas as they were experts at organization and discipline. Roman writings on rhetoric tend to bring together a variety of Greek ideas into an organized system, and in the teaching of rhetoric, the Romans contributed the methods of memorizing great speeches, and repeated practice to develop skill. Cicero, the greatest of all Roman orators, wrote seven books on the subject of rhetoric, drawing on a variety of Greek sources, but primarily relying on Aristotle (Clarke, 1953, p. 52). Cicero suggested that oratory has three practical objectives, "to instruct, to please, and to win over," all of which were vital to functioning as a citizen in a Roman republic (Clarke, 1953, p. 152).

Quintillian, whose approach to the study of rhetoric was always complex and detailed, steered students toward "declamation," the memorizing and performing of great speeches that had been given in the past, often speeches by Cicero. Quintillian lived and worked during the period of the Roman Empire, when Rome was autocratically ruled by emperors. He was more interested in rhetoric as a way to help build disciplined thought processes, and in speeches as performances that could inspire patriotic responses. During the later period of the empire, rhetoricians were popular figures at the emperor's court, and dramatic oratory was an honored art, but it was more a form of entertainment than a practical study aimed at influencing decisions (Clarke, 1953, pp. 130-131).

Rhetoric in Christian Europe

During the fourth and fifth centuries AD, Roman authority weakened and finally collapsed. The empire split into pieces; education outside the walls of Christian monasteries virtually ceased; classical knowledge and classical documents, even literacy were largely lost to Western Europe. In medieval Europe, the Roman Catholic Church replaced secular authority as the central organizing and civilizing influence.

Christianity can be considered a "rhetorical religion" in that it relies on preaching to win and to hold converts (Clarke, 1953, p. 130). On the other hand, Christianity relies on "divine revelation" as an authoritative source of doctrinal Truth. Hence, Christians, especially Church officials, preferred to view rhetoric as a tool for use by those who possess divinely revealed Truth in teaching and persuading converts. Rhetoric as a way to discover truth had no place in the Christian view.

Interestingly, St. Augustine, the great Christian writer and preacher in the fourth century AD, was educated to be a rhetorician before his conversion to Christianity. Augustine struggled with the place of his own education in his life as a Christian. While he retained his appreciation for well chosen words and well constructed phrases, Augustine sought to guide Christians away from materialistic concerns and toward spiritual consideration of their relationship to God. Hence, while he was himself a powerful writer and speaker, Augustine's influence on the study of rhetoric was negative. He took Plato's stance, suggesting that rhetoric could be used to help present Truth, but gave rhetoric no part in the pursuit of truth (Clarke, 1953, pp.; 150-153).

Christianity also had the effect of reducing focus on, and access to, the whole body of ancient knowledge, which was suspect in the minds of Christian leaders because it came from pagan sources, and often explicitly rested on pagan authority. As the Roman Empire disintegrated, Christian monasteries became the only places in Western Europe where literacy was taught, and where books were preserved. Pagan works, and works focused on worldly skills such as rhetoric tended not to be included. Western Europe lost most of its ancient knowledge. Some Roman works on rhetoric, which were based on Greek texts, were preserved, but the classic Greek works, including Aristotle's Rhetoric, were lost.

Key Contribution of the Moors

During the period when Europe lacked knowledge and centralized authorities, Islam took hold in the Middle East and in North Africa. As Muslims gained control in various areas, they tended to eagerly acquire whatever knowledge existing cultures could offer. The ancient library at Alexandria was a cherished and well-used institution in Muslim culture, as were the works of ancient Persian scholars. Thus, the period we call the "Dark Ages" in Europe was an intellectual, artistic, economic, and military golden age for Islam. Muslim scholars not only acquired the ancient European knowledge deposited at Alexandria, but also added significant contributions of their own in philosophy, mathematics, and architecture.

Militant Muslims known as the Moors invaded Spain in 711 AD, and dominated much of Spain for almost seven centuries. During those centuries Europeans fought in periodic campaigns to recover Spanish territory for Christianity. The city of Toledo served for many years as a Moorish capital in Spain, and the Moors established there a great library housing probably half a million books, most of which were copies of the works in the library at Alexandria, including Aristotle's and Plato's works. In 1085 AD, when Christian crusaders recaptured Toledo, the Moors retreated from the city leaving behind their library (Easton, 1966, p. 284).

Recognizing that the Moors possessed considerable knowledge which Christian Europeans lacked, the new Bishop of Toledo ordered that the books in the library be preserved and translated into Latin for the benefit of Europe (Easton, 1966, p. 284). Over the next four decades, Christian scholars, and a number of educated Jewish inhabitants of Toledo, labored to translate and copy the many works in the Moorish library. Copies of translated works were sent to Christian universities all over Europe. Among these works were Aristotle's writings, including the Rhetoric. It was this capturing of Muslim knowledge, and recapturing of its own knowledge, that enabled Europe to achieve its Renaissance (Easton, 1966, p. 284). Yet, interest and scholarship in rhetoric, while recognized and practiced, would not significantly advance again until the nineteenth century.

Christian scholars, especially at the University of Paris, became interested in ancient Greek philosophical works, and some suggested that Aristotle's work on logic could be used to help explain theological issues. Aristotle's work, however, was viewed by most as highly suspect, since he had been pagan, and these works came through the hands of the Muslims. The ideas of the Muslim philosopher, Averroes, were advocated by some Christian scholars. Averroes had argued that there are two kinds of knowledge, worldly and spiritual, and that while spiritual knowledge could come only through divine revelation, worldly knowledge could come from observation and reason (Easton, 1966, p. 173). With this argument, Averroes had secured permission to study secular texts that might disagree with Islamic teaching. Such thoughts, however, appeared to threaten Church authority in Christian Europe, and were officially disapproved (Easton, 1966, p. 284). Only after Thomas Aquinas, the great Parisian scholar and monk, showed that Aristotle's logic could serve well to support Christian teaching were ancient works given more serious study. And, among the ancient works studied, writings on rhetoric were very low on Christian scholars' lists of priorities (Easton, 1966, p. 285). The Roman Catholic Church was a highly autocratic structure, as were the monarchies that were establishing themselves in medieval Europe. The art of persuading individuals who were free to make rational choices was not particularly relevant in medieval Europe.

The Gradual Return of Democracy, and New Relevance for Rhetoric

During the medieval period, active study and practice of rhetoric continued in England and Europe, but the focus of this study was limited to providing direction and observation to the general populace (Howell, 1961, P. 64). For almost 800 years, rhetoric was studied and practiced with a "profound deference to authority," relying on studies of Cicero's speeches, Quintillian's observations on style, and formulating patterns for conveying information clearly (Howell, 1961, p. 65). Aristotle's direct influence entered the English study of rhetoric in 1551 with publication of a work by Thomas Wilson called Rule of Reason, but Wilson did not rely on Aristotle's *Rhetoric*. Rather, Wilson built his work on Aristotle's *Logic* (Howell, 1961, pp. 12-13).

England under the near absolute rule of monarchs was no place for a broad study of rhetoric to flourish. However, beginning in 1215 AD, when King John was forced to sign the Magna Carta, the English monarchy gradually surrendered power first to English nobles, then also to English commoners. By the nineteenth century, England had a "constitutional monarchy" in which the king shared authority with Parliament, and in Parliament issues were debated and voted upon. This relatively democratic form of government in nineteenth century England provided fertile soil for a resurgence of rhetorical study, theory, and practice. Moreover, as the Industrial Revolution developed, bringing with it the growth of a strong middle and professional class, England was fertile soil for broadening the study of human communication beyond the traditional boundaries of rhetoric.

Three important English scholars focused on rhetoric during the late 18th and early 19th centuries, and made significant new contributions for our understanding of the subject: George Campbell, Hugh Blair, and Richard Whately.

George Campbell added a strong psychological focus to our understanding of persuasion. In his book, Philosophy of Rhetoric, published in 1776, he suggested that rhetoric could be used to express ideas and create moods, as well as to argue rationally (Smith, 1998, p. 253). Campbell believed the "human psyche could be divided into the understanding, the will, the affections, the memory, and the imagination," and that these elements could be combined by the speaker to create a unified emotional response in an audience (Smith, 1998, p. 253). Campbell gave rhetoric a much broader purpose than the mere reporting of established Truth. He said the purposes of rhetoric were to "enlighten the understanding, to awaken the memory, to engage the imagination, to arouse the passions to influence the will to action or belief" (Smith, 1998, p. 254). Campbell's psychological approach, and his broader view of the purposes of rhetoric were highly influential.

Hugh Blair appreciated the artistic aspects as well as the influence aspects of rhetoric, and he taught and lectured on the subject throughout his adult life. The collection of forty-seven of his lectures on the subject published in 1783 as a book entitled *Lectures on Rhetoric and Belles Lettres*, was very widely read in both England and the United States (Smith, 1998, p. 256). Blair preached that it was critically important to exercise correct taste in speaking. He argued that ultimately, it is emotion, not reason, that drives human action, and be believed with Campbell that emotions aroused in an audience could be contagious (Smith, 1998, p. 257).

Richard Whately is notable for advancing both democracy and rhetorical thought. Whately was the Anglican archbishop of Saint Patrick's Cathedral in Dublin, Ireland. When he became a member of Parliament, however, he strongly advocated emancipation of Irish Catholics from British dominance (Smith, 1998, p. 261). Whately was particularly interested in the use of reason in persuasion, and he viewed logic as a tool of rhetoric. In his handbook, *The Elements of Rhetoric*, first published in 1828, he utilized his own translation of Aristotle's ideas to develop the modern study of argumentation (Smith, 1998, p. 261). Whately's work on the theory of argument stood as the definitive theory for more than a century.

During this same period, the study of rhetoric was also a thriving enterprise in America. American universities included rhetoric as an important element in their curricula. Although early American rhetoricians were less influential than their English counterparts, they nevertheless made visible contributions to the study. John Witherspoon, one of the signers of the Declaration of Independence, was Professor of Rhetorical Studies at Princeton. In 1800, Witherspoon published *Lectures on Moral Philosophy and Eloquence*, the first complete treatise on rhetoric written in America (Becker, 1989). Before becoming President, John Quincy Adams served as Professor of Rhetoric and Oratory at Harvard. Adams' book, *Lectures on Rhetoric and Oratory*, was published in 1810 (Becker, 1989). Noah Webster's son-in-law, Chauncey Goodrich, who was Professor of Rhetoric at Yale from 1817 to 1839, published a collection of analyses of British orators. Goodrich's work, titled *Select British Eloquence*, established the model followed by later historical studies of influential speakers, and continued to serve as an important rhetorical criticism text into the mid-twentieth century (Becker, 1989).

Broadening the Study of Communication: Elocutionary Thought

Development of democracy opened the way for the study of rhetoric to fully develop in England and in the United States during the eighteenth century. The Industrial Revolution and the rise of a middle class provided the ground for a broadening of the study of human communication. One reason why Hugh Blair's work on "belles lettres" became so popular in both England and the United States was that a large and growing number of people were moving from the peasant class into the new middle class. Middle class people needed to learn how to present themselves properly in polite company, and Blair's focus on proper taste in the use of language provided very helpful advice. Still, learning to present oneself properly was a significant task, and two important writers, Thomas Sheridan and Gilbert Austin provided an approach to address this need, advocating what they called "elocution."

Thomas Sheridan was a famous English actor in the eighteenth century who came to believe that by learning the principles of proper pronunciation, correct posture, and graceful movement which actors learned, people could learn to present themselves well in polite society. In his book, *A Course of Lectures on Elocution*, published in 1762, he introduced the principles of elocution and offered the important new insight that the spoken word has significant properties which the written word does not have (Smith, 1998, p. 259).

Gilbert Austin, drew heavily upon the work of Sheridan and Blair, as well as upon classical rhetoric, to develop a detailed theory of elocution, which was published in his work, *A Treatise on Rhetorical Delivery*, in 1806 (Smith, 1998, p. 259). Sheridan's and Austin's ideas form the basis of the study of elocution which flourished throughout the nineteenth and early twentieth centuries in England and the United States. Among their followers was Henry Ward, an English elocution teacher who claimed that by changing the way one spoke, he could change one's entire personality. Henry Ward served as the model for the fictional character Henry Higgins in *My Fair Lady*, and the plot of *My Fair Lady* is based upon Ward's ideas.

By the beginning of the twentieth century, elocution was widely taught throughout England and the United States. If one intended to function in the middle class as a merchant or as a professional, or as the spouse of a professional, one was generally expected to study with an elocution instructor, and to master the art of presenting oneself and one's ideas properly. In English and American colleges and universities, the study of rhetoric was taught in English departments, and focused on effective written arguments and essays. Elocution instructors were typically not members of college faculties, but were private teachers who located near colleges. To be educated, one not only went to college; one also took private lessons in elocution.

The Academic Discipline of Speech Communication

During the early decades of the twentieth century, elocution instructors gradually joined college faculties as members of English departments, and their instruction was offered through the college as "Elocution," or "Voice and Diction," or "Speech." Elocution instructors typically shared an interest and expertise in theater as well, and taught acting, and directed college plays. As members of academic institutions, however, they soon came to view their field not as a subset of English, but as a distinct and separate study. In 1910 a group of public speaking teachers broke from the National Council of Teachers of English to form their own professional organization (Leff & Procario, 1985). By 1915 they had established their own separate professional association, the Speech Association of America (SAA), and had begun publication of their own academic journals. During the 1920s and 1930s they succeeded in establishing their own academic departments,

ments, most often called Departments of Speech or, joined with theater, Departments of Speech and Theater. Drawing on their intellectual heritage from the sophists to Gilbert Austin, they constructed a body of theory, and developed a coherent curriculum of courses. Their courses typically covered development of rhetorical theory from Aristotle to the present, public speaking, voice and diction, argumentation, debate, and group discussion. In the tradition of the sophists and Aristotle, their focus was on training students in the communication skills needed to function effectively as a citizen in a democracy.

As their focus broadened to include interpersonal communication, small group communication, organizational communication, and mass communication; and their methods expanded to draw upon social science research, these departments changed their names to Speech Communication, and, later Communication Studies, or simply Communication. At the University of Arizona, the old wooden sign over the door of our building reads "Speech;" the modern sign standing in front of the building reads "Communication." The two signs stand like book ends, with two important volumes in the history of communication study between them. One volume is the story of the modern discipline of rhetoric; the other is the story of the social science of communication. We tell those two stories in Chapters 3 and 4.

References

Becker, S. L. (1989). The rhetorical tradition. In S. S. King (Ed.), *Human communication as a field of study* (pp. 27-41). Albany, NY: State University of New York Press.

Clarke, M. L. (1953). *Rhetoric at Rome*. London: Cohen & West, Ltd.

Easton, S. C. (1966). *The western heritage* (2nd ed.). New York: Holt, Rinehart, and Winston, Inc.

Howell, W. S. (1961). *Logic and rhetoric in England, 1500-1700*. New York: Russell & Russell, Inc.

Leff, M. C. & Procario, M. O. (1985). Rhetorical theory in speech communication. In T. W. Benson (Ed.), *Speech communication in the twentieth century* (pp. 3-27). Carbondale and Edwardsville, IL: Southern Illinois University Press.

Smith, C. (1998). *Rhetoric and human consciousness: A history*. Prospect Heights, IL: Waveland Press, Inc.

Chapter 3
Rhetoric and Speech in 20ᵗʰ Century American Universities

When we say that Communication is a 2500-year old discipline, we use the term *discipline*, in the broad sense, meaning *a systematic study* or *an organized body of knowledge about a subject.* During the nineteenth century, however, the term *academic discipline* acquired a narrower, more precise definition, which specified two criteria for determining whether a study area should be considered a discipline. Those criteria were:

1. The content must be a substantial and discrete subject area that is not covered by any other discipline; and
2. The discipline must have a methodology of its own, that is, an accepted set of systematic methods for developing new knowledge about its subject.

Given this narrower definition, there was considerable question as to whether the study of human communication could qualify as a modern academic discipline.

During the late nineteenth century, American colleges and universities organized themselves into organizational units called *departments*, dividing scholars into academic groups representing disciplines. In an academic world organized according to established disciplines, scholars and teachers whose subjects were speech and rhetoric struggled to carve out a secure platform for their work. As they separated from English departments and sought to define their place in the academic community these scholars faced four difficult problems:

1. They were latecomers as a modern academic discipline.
2. Their subject matter was academically suspect.
3. They lacked an articulated methodology.
4. They labored in Plato's Shadow.

Each of these problems is briefly described below.

1. As representatives of an academic discipline, Speech Communication scholars arrived about twenty years late on the American academic scene, emerging from English departments in the 19-teens and twenties. Scholars in philosophy, English, mathematics, and the physical sciences had by that time been engaged for several decades in defining the nature and scope of their scholarly work; each of their studies was already established as a discipline. Psychology and Sociology, the most recent additions to the academy had credibly advanced their claims to status as disciplines at the turn of the century. Thus, despite their 2500-year history, in the American academy, speech communication scholars represented a fledgling discipline, seeking recognition among established disciplines.
2. The subject of their study was either not substantial, or not discrete. Communication, as the elocutionists had taught it, was purely a matter of process; there seemed to be no *content* to the subject. Communication does not occur unless a message with some content is communicated. However, when the *content* of communication was viewed as part of the subject, as in the Aristotelian approach to rhetoric, the subject matter was no longer discrete; it overlapped with politics, literature, economics, psychology, sociology, and any number of other

subjects. Thus, early twentieth century communication scholars confronted a dilemma in attempting to establish their work as a modern academic discipline. If they defined their subject narrowly enough to be discrete, it lacked substance. If they defined their subject as including the content of communication, their subject was no longer discrete.

3. Scholars in speech communication had no methodology of their own. Scholars in established disciplines had been busy for decades discussing and achieving broad agreement concerning the systematic processes by which their subjects should be studied. No such discussion had occurred among nineteenth elocutionists or rhetoricians. The work of developing a methodology was still in front of the communication scholars in the early twentieth century, and they would not be able to claim full status as a modern academic discipline until it could be completed.

4. Plato's Shadow served to undermine their credibility as they struggled to make their case. Like the sophists in ancient Greece, the teachers of public speaking were purveyors of a practical art. At best, their efforts yielded good speeches, but the skills they taught could also be employed to make falsehoods appear true. At best, the outcomes of their work were products (speeches) which, although they were clearly valuable when used to promote good outcomes, were not comparable to the discoveries of enduring truths which were the ideal outcomes of established academic efforts. Thus, their colleagues in English and philosophy could evoke Plato's Shadow, accusing them of lacking real interest in the any enduring body of knowledge. In the twentieth century, as in ancient Athens, the rhetorician's work seemed tainted by doubts about its relationship to the pursuit of truth.

Given these four daunting problems, it is not surprising that speech communication scholars have struggled to "chart the history [of their discipline], to define its nature and scope, to determine its relationships to other domains of learning, and to conceive the foundation on which it might rest" (Leff & Procario, 1985). Neither is it surprising that speech communication scholars would differ among themselves in their responses to such fundamental issues as "What should be the scope of our study?" Or, "What principles should be considered foundational in building our scholarly method?" As early twentieth century communication scholars addressed these basic issues, one group sought to build its study on the foundation of classical rhetoric, and to focus on *speech* as public address. Another group sought to ally itself with the new social sciences of psychology and sociology, and to focus on the *human behavior of speaking* as its subject. Although these two approaches were not incompatible, there was (and is) considerable rivalry and tension between them.

Another challenging issue was the question of what this modern study of communication should be called. "Public Speaking," the label adopted by public speaking teachers when they formed their own professional association in 1910, was clearly too narrow. "Rhetoric"as a label clearly excluded the scholars who advocated a broader scope for their study. The term "speech," however, was a conveniently ambiguous and inclusive label that could be reasonably applied to both the rhetorical and the social science approaches. So, the first label for the modern study of communication became "Speech." The Speech Association of America was formed in 1915 as the national organization for professional academicians who studied communication. In colleges and universities where the new discipline was recognized, academic units labeled *Department of Speech*, or (when combined with scholars focusing on drama) *Department of Speech and Theater* were established to conduct research and provide instruction concerning human communication.

Neo-Aristotelian Scholarship

In this chapter we describe the ideas, methods, and contributions of the scholars who based their work on classical rhetorical concepts, and built the rhetorical approach to the modern discipline Speech Communication. The primary architects of the rhetorical approach to communication study were a group of scholars at Cornell University including James Winans, Alexander Drummond, Everett Hunt, Harry Caplan, Herbert Wichelns, and Hoyt Hudson (Leff & Procario, 1985). This group, who came to be called the Cornell School, built their study and a coherent curriculum of courses on a foundation of classical rhetorical theory, primarily upon the work of Aristotle. They placed their study among the humanities, adopted the sophists' lofty goal of teaching *arrete*, aiming to provide students with the communication skills they needed to function as effective citizens in both public and private life. They placed oratory, the public speech with political impact, at the center of their study, and labeled the skills they taught as "tools of a democracy" (Ewbank and Auer, 1941).

In adopting the sophists' ideal of *arrete*, and viewing their subject as an essential democratic tool, the Cornell School committed themselves to including both the content and the processes of speech making in their study. They noted that *invention*, the first of Aristotle's five canons of rhetoric, focused on developing the content of a speech, and that the *topoi* among which Aristotle taught his students to search for ideas and issues were in the domains of politics, poetry, history, and psychology (Leff & Procario, 1985). So, if inclusion of speech content in their subject matter meant that theirs was not a fully discrete subject, so be it. Grounding their study in Aristotle's *Rhetoric*, they asserted an ancient claim to the territory.

While acknowledging some shared subject matter with other disciplines, the Cornell School advanced the case for treating rhetoric as a separate discipline from English through a series of articles published during the nineteen twenties. The most influential of these articles was an essay by Herbert Wichelns entitled "The Literary Criticism of Oratory" (1925). Wichelns clearly pointed out key differences between the rhetorical critic and the literary critic. He noted that while the literary critic's interest was in works that artistically spoke universal truths to all audiences in all times, the rhetorical critic's interest was in how effectively a specific speaker communicated with a *specific* audience, in a specific time, place, and context. He acknowledged the presence of aspects of poetry and literature in good rhetoric, but he clearly distinguished rhetoric from literature in terms of its focus and purpose. Noting how Aristotle distinguished rhetoric from logic on the one hand, and from poetic on the other, Wichelns and other proponents of the Cornell School adopted classical rhetorical concepts in general, and Aristotle's *Rhetoric* in particular, as the theoretical foundation of their study.

Neo-Aristotelian Methods

Over the next two decades rhetoricians at Cornell, and at several Midwestern universities developed methodological details and standards, and adopted fairly standardized graduate and undergraduate curricula for the rhetorically based study of communication. The methodology of rhetorical criticism based primarily upon Aristotle's concepts came to be called Neo-Aristotelian Criticism. In its mature form, it was fully described by Lester Thonnsen and A. Craig Baird (1948) in *Speech Criticism*. First published in 1948, *Speech Criticism* stood for two decades as the standard methodological text for rhetorical criticism. Applying these critical methods to important speakers and speeches in history, Neo-Aristotelian scholars produced significant histories of public address in the United States and England. William Norwood

Brigance, for example, served as editor to produce an extensive, multi-volume *History of American Public Address* (1943).

Neo-Aristotelian rhetorical critics employed Aristotle's and other classical treatises as theoretical bases for analyzing and evaluating specific speeches and speakers. The central questions these scholars sought to answer were drawn from Aristotle's definition of rhetoric, "the art of discovering all the available means of persuasion in a given situation." Assuming with Aristotle that a speech was an intentional effort to bring about a change in a specific audience, for a specific purpose, in a specific time, place, and context, they sought to understand whether and how a speaker adapted to all the specific conditions, and employed specific means of persuasion to achieve his or her purpose. As a first step, they would systematically gather all information available about the audience and the context. Secondly, they would gather all available information concerning the speaker that might shed light on his/her purpose in speaking, or his/her available means of persuasion. Third, they would carefully study the verbal text of the speech, and any descriptive material they could find about the how the speech was delivered, or how the audience responded. Then, they would analyze the speech text in light of all the other information they had gathered to determine how the speaker accomplished his/her ethical, emotional, and logical appeals to the audience. They also studied the text of the speech to describe and evaluate the ideas employed by the speaker (invention), the organizational patterns (organization), stylistic devices in the language used (style). They examined descriptions of the speech and the speaker (or, later, recordings and pictures) to describe and evaluate the delivery. Based upon these descriptions and analyses, they drew conclusions about whether, how, and why specific speakers on specific occasions were able to influence their audiences.

These rhetorical critics did not seek to draw general conclusions about the nature of speech making. Nor did they engage in literary or artistic analysis. There efforts are best classified as specialized historical studies, since they viewed each speech as a unique event occurring in an historical context, and sought to develop better understanding of each speech as an historical event. They conducted systematic, theory-based, objective research, and added much to our understanding of important speeches as historical events. Secondarily, their work provided insights and models that have proved very useful in developing public speaking instruction.

Not all Neo-Aristotelian scholars focused on critically evaluating speeches. Some devoted themselves to carefully and completely understanding classical, medieval, and modern rhetorical theories. George Kennedy's study of Greek rhetorical theory (1963), and W. S. Howell's investigation of English rhetorical thought (1961) are excellent examples of these scholarly efforts.

The Neo-Aristotelian Curriculum

Curricula developed by Neo-Aristotelian scholars for studying Speech Communication included:

1. Study of rhetorical theory, beginning with classical Greek and Roman works and including the English rhetoricians, Campbell, Whately, and Blair. Primary attention was given to the study of Aristotle's *Rhetoric.*
2. Studies of the methodology of rhetorical criticism, and application of rhetorical criticism as a way to better understand speeches and speech making. The primary method for critically analyzing speeches was to evaluate their effectiveness by examining how well speakers accomplished ethical, logical, and emotional appeals to the audience (Aristotle's artistic proofs of ethos, logos and pathos), and by studying how speak-

ers enacted Aristotle's five canons of invention, disposition, style, memory and delivery.

3. Historical studies of English and American public address, which examined and evaluated speakers and speeches of apparent historical importance. Historical speakers and speeches were critically analyzed using Aristotle's concepts of ethos, logos and pathos, and the five canons.

4. Study and skill development in public speaking. Students learned and practiced giving persuasive speeches, informative speeches, and ceremonial speeches. Here again, the fundamental concepts were drawn from Aristotle. Examples and models were often drawn from historical speeches.

5. Study and skill development in argumentation and debate. This subject area included development of intercollegiate competition in debate and other speaking activities. Until 1961, the concepts and principles used to define good argument were based primarily on Richard Whately's nineteenth century work.

6. Study and skill development in small group discussion, which entered course catalogs mostly during the 1930's as a more cooperatively democratic alternative to the verbal combat of debate. For this subject, speech communication scholars were required to develop more original content. They drew heavily upon the underlying principles of parliamentary procedure, on democratic principles of egalitarianism, and on Thomas Dewey's rational model for problem solving.

7. Study and skill development in the performance of great historical speeches (known as "oratorical declamation") and oral interpretation of poetry and literature. These practices reflected the influence of the Roman rhetorician Quintillian, and the association of Speech with drama and theater.

8. Study and skill development in vocal expression, usually called "voice and diction." These courses reflected the elocutionists' perspective, and were also useful for drama students.

Alternative Approaches

The Cornell School's Neo-Aristotelian approach, with its focus on public speeches, was widely adopted in Midwestern universities and colleges, and became the dominant approach to communication study from about 1925 to about 1965. However, it was never the *only* approach. The social science perspective advocated by Charles Woolbert and other Midwestern scholars in the 19-teens and twenties, focused not on speech making, but on the act of speaking, which they regarded as a uniquely human behavior. This perspective remained an influence, and grew significantly stronger through the 1940s and 1950s. Nor was Neo-Aristotelianism the only recognized method of rhetorical criticism. Recognizing the limitations of Neo-Aristotelianism, rhetoricians began to develop alternative methods for analyzing speeches.

Marie Hochmuth Nichols, a leading rhetorical critic and scholar, was especially active in pursuing alternative methodological approaches. She extensively studied the work of philosopher Kenneth Burke, and demonstrated how his metaphorical use of five aspects of drama could be applied to analyze persuasive messages (Nichols, 1963). She pointed out to Speech Communication scholars how Burke's *Dramatistic Pentad* could serve as a "critical apparatus" to determine how a speaker achieved *identity* with an audience, thus persuading them to her/his point of view. Nichols also showed how the ideas of I. A. Richards, a British scholar, could be used by critics to better determine the full meaning of any message (Nichols, 1963).

Other rhetorical scholars developed original methodological approaches that were better suited than Aristotelian criticism for addressing their particular scholarly interests. Below are some important examples:

• Observing that social change was often accomplished through social and political movements which were active over time, and which might include hundreds of speeches as well as many other symbolic acts, Leland Griffin (1952) developed and applied a method for rhetorically analyzing such movements. This method was applied both to historical movements, such as the abolition movement, and to contemporary movements, such as the Civil Rights Movement, or the campaign against the Viet Nam War.

- Ernest Bormann (1972) developed a process he called "fantasy theme analysis" (which later evolved into symbolic convergence theory) to better identify and define the persuasive messages embedded in narratives. In developing fantasy theme analysis, Bormann explicitly recognized that some realities are "socially constructed." His concept of "rhetorical vision" described the social reality that develops when a shared, common set of fantasy themes is voiced among many people. Social realities become and remain realities simply and only because people agree that they are real.

- Lloyd Bitzer (1968) developed a systematic process for analyzing the situational context of a speech, providing a method for rhetorical critics to examine an important aspect of any speech that had not been adequately addressed in Aristotle's work. Bitzer's work was particularly useful in providing a method for understanding how a specific speaker's options are limited and constrained by emerging situational factors.

The End of the Neo-Aristotelian Era

Neo-Aristotelian scholarship represents an important developmental era in the modern study of communication. Neo-Aristotelian scholars conducted valuable research and contributed useful insights concerning speech, speeches, and social change, but in harnessing their efforts to Greek and Roman ideas, and in focusing tightly on public address, they severely limited the scope and the utility of their study. So, Neo-Aristotelian dominance in communication study was bound to be time-limited. We date the period of Neo-Aristotelian rhetorical study from 1925, when Wichelns' article distinguishing rhetorical criticism from literary criticism was first published, to 1965, when a book by Edwin Black on rhetorical criticism clearly pointed out the limitations of Neo-Aristolian scholarship (1965). Three significant developments helped bring about the end of the Neo-Aristotelian era: (1) the rise of Hitler, (2) the rise of postmodernism, and (3) the rise of social science. Below, we briefly explain how each of these developments altered the study of communication.

The Rise of Hitler

Hitler's ascent to power in Germany, and the horrendous crimes he and his lieutenants perpetrated with that power, shook the foundations of trust in democratic governance. Hitler came to power through *democratic processes* in Germany, and he gained and retained broad support among the German people through persuasion. In part, he held power because he was an *extremely effective orator*. Hitler demonstrated the deeply disturbing fact that skill in persuasive oratory can be used to do terrible harm. He embodied the "dark side of communication," which we discussed in Chapter 1. Observing what Hitler had wrought, many rhetorical scholars became uncomfortably uncertain about the merits of developing and teaching knowledge and skills for persuasion. It was obviously important to also focus on finding ways to ensure that persuasion would be used only for social good.

The Development of Postmodernism

Postmodernism, as a general movement, began in the field of architecture. In the flurry of rebuilding and new building after World War II, architects used the term "modern" to signify an architectural style that focused on functional construction at minimal cost. Recognizing that "modern" buildings were drab and uninspiring, Philip Johnson, a leading American architect, advocated and began designing what he called "postmodern" buildings. Postmodern buildings were designed to reflect their local environments, and to inspire. Once expressed and embodied as architecture, the idea of postmodernism spread quickly through the American and European intellectual communities (Smith, 1998).

Postmodernists argued that societies damaged themselves by over-relying on science and technology. They were deeply suspicions of social science as an approach. They argued that we live in world fragmented into to very different cultures, with differing systems of "truth," and the claim of science to produce a single Truth was bogus. Much of what passes for truth, they suggested, is culture based. The mechanism for building cultures is rhetoric, and the questions of who controls the rules of rhetoric, how, and to what end, are of primary importance.

Key thinkers whose ideas provided an intellectual foundaton for postmodern thought about communication included Richard Weaver, Jergen Habermas, Michael Foucault, and Jean-Francois Lyotard. In the early 1950s, Weaver articulated the fundamental notions that cultures are made of ideas, that ideas can literally "dominate" people's lives, and that even "tyrannical" ideas can be addressed and changed (Weaver, 1953). Jergen Habermas, the post World War II German scholar who sought to build a set of critical methods that would prevent the rise of harmful totalitarian governments, provided the key idea that people can and must liberate themselves by critically evaluating the content of their culture (Smith, 1998). For Habermas, the fundamental purpose of rhetorical criticism was *liberation*, and the primary purpose for understanding persuasion was to defend oneself against it. During the 1960s and 1970s, Michael Foucault, a brilliant French scholar, convincingly showed that fundamental power in any culture is wielded through control of the rules of communication (Smith, 1998). Jean-Franciose Lyotard focused attention on the fact that our perception of reality is organized through our language, and that language (and therefore perceptions of reality) vary by culture (Smith, 1998).

To feminist scholars postmodernism offered an intellectual platform on which to build their case showing the impact on women of a reality system created by men. A host of feminist scholars took on an intense critique of American and other cultures, exposing the many direct and subtle ways cultures defined by men have limited women's roles and oppressed women as a class. Feminist rhetorical critics energized and brought important insights to the postmodern approach.

Whether or not they use the term, postmodern scholars focus intensely on rhetoric. Their interest, however, is not in *whether* a message is effective, but in *what effect* the message produces. They were concerned with the contents and outcomes of messages. Many of these scholars had (and have) an explicitly political agenda to which they were (and are) passionately committed. They focus their critical efforts on interpreting meanings and outcomes of messages, and assessing their merits accordingly. They are especially interested in how power is exercised through *control of the rules of rhetoric and language*. They view the Neo-Aristotelians' focus on specific arguments and persuasive techniques, and the social scientists' generalizations about specific communication behaviors, as extremely superficial and culture bound. From a postmodern intellectual perspective, Neo-Aristotelian rhetorical theory and criticism have very limited relevance.

The Rise of Social Science

Social scientists seek to explain, to predict, and, based upon their explanations and predictions, to influence human behavior. Beginning in the late nineteenth century, and continuing through the first half of the twentieth century, social scientists steadily refined their focus, and improved their methods of study until, by the late 1940s they were beginning to deliver knowledge that clearly did improve the quality of human life. As the social sciences demonstrated their utility and became more credible, they drew scholars away from other approaches. Social psychologists and sociologists included studies of human communication in their efforts and, especially in the areas of interpersonal, small group, and mass communication, provided significant advances in our understanding. As Speech Communication scholars noticed, and began to apply social science research and theory in their own work, the study of communication in Departments of Speech was profoundly changed in two ways: (1) social science methods began to supplant rhetorical criticism in their scholarly work; and (2) the scope of communication study was broadened to include *all* communication, while the focus on public speaking was proportionately reduced. It was in response to the incorporation of social science in their work that Departments of Speech began changing their names to Speech Communication, or Communication Studies, or, simply, Communication. The Speech Association of America changed its name to the Speech Communication Association and, very recently, to the National Communication Association. These were not mere name changes; they reflected a fundamental shift the way communication scholars defined in the nature and scope of communication study. They signaled the end of the Neo-Aristotelian era.

Edwin Black's Book

The single event that most clearly marked the end of the Neo-Aristotelian dominance in communication study was the publication in 1965 of Edwin Black's book entitled *Rhetorical Criticism: A Study of Method.* In this small but influential volume, Black offered three reasons why rhetorical critics should reach beyond Neo-Aristotelianism to find other methods:

First, he pointed out that speeches represent only a tiny percentage of human communication, even a tiny percentage of rhetorical communication, and that speeches were hardly the most important aspect of human communication. Clearly, the scope of critical study needed to be vastly enlarged.

Second, he noted that if one is interested in determining whether a speech (or any other communication) is effective, social science offers far better methods than Neo-Aristotelian criticism. He suggested that communication scholars seeking to determine the effects of speeches should conduct survey research among the speech audiences. Since social science methods offered a way to directly measure effects of speeches, contrived analytic methods which produced judgments about possible effects were simply outmoded.

Finally, Black argued that effectiveness was not the only consideration in evaluating a speech. To drive home this point, he pointed to the example of the Coatesville Address, a commemorative speech given in 1912, at Coatesville, Pennsylvania to mark the anniversary of a brutal lynching of a Black man in that town. The speaker, John J. Chapman, delivered his address because he believed the anniversary of that terrible event should not pass unremembered and unmarked. Although he had advertised the speech in the newspaper and with posters, and rented the town hall for the occasion, Chapman spoke to an audience of one. Other than the speaker, only one person attended the Coatesville Address—a reporter for the local newspaper who had been assigned to report on the event. The speech, however, was eloquent and profoundly moving in its clear moral condemnation of racism and violence. Black produced the entire text of Chapman's speech, and challenged any of his fellow rhetorical critics to say that this was not an important or successful address, though it had clearly not persuaded the unrepentant citizens of Coatesville. Not one scholar challenged Black's argument; effectiveness was clearly not an appropriate measure for this speech.

After 1965, publication of Neo-Aristotelian critical analyses dropped off sharply, replaced by postmodern critical studies of messages and movements, and by social scientific studies of communication processes. Social scientific study focused more on interpersonal communication and on mass media messages than on speeches. Critical analyses focused more on interpreting the content of mass media. Communication scholars interested in practical application rather than theory development began focusing more on applying communication research in specific contexts such as organization management, small group problem solving, or health promotion. The scope and emphasis of communication curricula and instruction shifted accordingly.

The Neo-Aristotelian Legacy

The Neo-Aristotelian era ended about thirty years ago, but the scholarship it produced has by no means disappeared from the study of human communication. We see at least five ways in which Neo-Aristotelianism continues to strongly influence our discipline.

1. Public speaking, the central interest of Neo-Aristotelian scholars, continues to be the most commonly taught and most widely enrolled communication course in American colleges and universities. Skill in public speaking continues to be clearly recognized as an important requisite for college graduates. Any review of the textbooks used or the syllabi of public speaking courses will clearly show that their content is based primarily on the rhetorical concepts distilled from Aristotle's *Rhetoric* by Neo-Aristotelian scholars.
2. Rhetorical criticism is a thriving, in fact growing, domain of scholarly activity. Postmodern critics rarely utilize direct applications of Aristotle's theories, but they certainly employ Wichelns' focus on understanding the impact of a specific communicator, on a specific audience, in a specific place and context. The intellectual roots of the postmodern critique of contemporary cultures and rhetoric include many sources other

than Neo-Aristotelian critics. Still, it is fair to say that Neo-Aristotelian critics provided important parts of the foundation upon which twentieth century communication scholars could build and apply new critical methods.

3. Argumentation and debate continue to thrive as domains of scholarly activity. The field of argumentation was revitalized in the early 1960's with publication of Stephen Toulmin's (1958) study of *The Uses of Argument.* Applying Toulmin's model of argument, scholars have dissected and insightfully analyzed a great variety of contemporary arguments. It is also noteworthy that intercollegiate competition in debate continues to provide students with a valuable means of building their skills in critical thinking and persuasion.

4. The ancient sophists' ideal of *arrete*, which views the purpose of education as helping students build the skills necessary for a useful public and private life, remains an influential criterion in making decisions about Communication curricula. Communication departments continue to design and offer courses with clear practical value. Work by communication scholars in organizational communication, health communication, and intercultural communication demonstrates contemporary application of the ideal of *arrete*, which Neo-Aristotelian scholars articulated for the twentieth century. In each of these areas of specialized communication study, direct, useful application of communication research is a central focus.

5. Finally, the intellectual foundation for many contemporary theories of social influence can be traced to Aristotelian concepts, definitions, and principles of rhetoric. The Neo-Aristotelian scholars were responsible for bringing Aristotle's ideas about communication into the 20th century.

References

Bitzer, L. (1968). The rhetorical situation. *Philosophy and Rhetoric, 1*, 1-14.

Black, E. (1965). *Rhetorical criticism: A study in method.* New York: Macmillan.

Bormann, E. (1972). Fantasy and rhetorical vision: the rhetorical criticism of social reality. *Quarterly Journal of Speech, 58,* 396-407.

Brigance, W. N. (1943). *A history and criticism of American public address.* New York: McGraw-Hill.

Brock, L. E. & Scott, R. L. (Eds.). (1980). *Methods of rhetorical criticism: A twentieth century perspective (2nd ed).* Detroit: Wayne State University Press.

Enos, R. L. (1985). The history of rhetoric: The reconstruction of progress. In T. W. Benson (Ed.), *Speech communication in the 20th century* (pp. 28-40). Carbondale and Edwardsville: Southern Illinois University Press.

Ewbank, H. L. & Auer, J. J. (1951). *Discussion and Debate: Tools of a democracy.* New York: Appleton-Century-Crofts.

Griffin, L. (1952). The rhetoric of historical movements. *The Quarterly Journal of Speech, XXXVIII,* 2.

Kennedy, G. (1963). *The art of persuasion in Greece.* Princeton, New Jersey: Princeton University Press.

Leff, M. C. & Procario, M. O. (1985). Rhetorical theory in speech communication. In T.W. Benson (Ed), *Speech communication in the 20th century* (pp. 3-27). Carbondale and Edwardsville: Southern Illinois University Press.

Nichols, M. H. (1963). *Rhetoric and criticism.* Baton Rouge: Louisiana State University Press.

Smith, C. R. (1998). *Rhetoric and human consciousness: A history.* Prospect Heights, Illinois: Waveland Press.

Thonnsen, L. & Baird, A. C. (1948). *Speech criticism.* New York: Ronald Press.

Toulmin, S. (1958). *The uses of argument.* Cambridge, England: Cambridge University Press.

Weaver R. (1953). *The Ethics of Rhetoric.* Chicago: Henry Regnery Company.

Wichelns, H. A. (1925). The literary criticism of oratory. In A. M. Drummond (Ed), *Studies in rhetoric and public speaking in honor of James A Winans.* New York: Century.

Chapter 4
The Emerging Social Science of Communication Study

In advocating that the study of human communication be approached as a social science, Charles Woolbert represented a minority view among early twentieth century speech scholars. Still, Woolbert stuck to his position, publishing the first known experiment to explicitly test a theory of persuasion in 1920 (Becker, 1989). In the fifty years that followed his first experimental study of persuasion, Woolbert's view was gradually adopted by a majority of communication scholars. However, during the decades when Neo-Aristotelian rhetoricians dominated the discipline of speech communication, it was scholars in other disciplines concerned with human social behavior who pioneered the development of the social scientific study of communication. Four of these important innovators, Harold Lasswell, Kurt Lewin, Paul Lazarsfeld, and Carl Hovland, were social scientists. A fifth pioneer, Wilbur Schramm, whose home discipline was English, pursued an explicitly interdisciplinary approach to the study. As social scientific study of communication matured during the 1950's, 60's and 70's, it was embraced by speech communication scholars, and given a natural home in speech communication departments.

In this chapter we trace the historical development of social scientific communication study during the twentieth century. To comprehend this development, it is important to understand the nature of social science, and how it differs from the rhetorical approach to studying communication. So, we begin the chapter with a brief explanation of the assumptions, characteristics, and practices of social science.

The Nature of Social Science

Scientific method assumes there is one enduring reality, or universal truth of human experience, which can be discovered by observing sensory data. The methods of social science, which are designed to objectively observe sensory data, are assumed to be sufficient to adequately explain that singular reality or truth. Social scientists assume that human behavior is governed by persistent rules or laws, and they seek to explain human behavior by systematically identifying those rules and laws. They are not interested in explaining unique events, single cases, individual behavior, or historical context; they are interested drawing general conclusions that explain patterns of aggregate behavior (Babbie, 1986, p. 20). Science is a logical, systematic method of investigation and analysis designed to explain natural phenomena. *Social science* attempts to find the best explanation for human behavior. It reaches this explanation through the process of scientific inquiry. Social scientists use scientific methods of inquiry to systematically observe human behavior, and to explain it.

Scientific inquiry protects against the mistakes and inaccuracies people tend to make in their informal, day-to-day explanations for why things are the way they are. We humans are prone to making many types of errors as we seek to explain things. These errors may be due to observing things inaccurately, reasoning illogically, overgeneralizing, observing selectively to avoid evidence that contradicts our ideas, being ego-involved in seeing things a certain way, and drawing premature conclusions, to name a just few (Babbie, pp. 6-16). To protect against these errors, inaccuracies and personal biases, social science research has a variety of built-in protective measures. These protections include: (a) the use of explicit logical reasoning; (b) committing in advance to a fixed method of observing and a fixed set of observations regardless of the results; (c) *replication*, or repeating studies using the same methods in different circumstances; (d) controlling for personal biases which may affect observations; and (e) peer review—the practice of having other scholars judge the merits of one's research. Thus, social science is conservative in its practices. Before any research findings are accepted as knowledge by the scientific community, they must follow accepted methods which minimize error and bias, and they must pass the critical review of other scholars.

Characteristics of Social Science

1. Social science aims for **objectivity** (standardization which is free from personal bias) in observations and conclusions. Objectivity provides the neutral common ground necessary to build knowledge. Although complete objectivity is an ideal that humans can only approximate, scientific method provides the logic and procedures that allow researchers with differing views to agree that reality has been accurately observed. Given objectivity, replications of a study should yield the same results (Littlejohn, 1999, p. 10).

2. Social science aims to be **descriptive, not prescriptive**. Science is concerned with knowing accurately how and why social phenomena occur. That is, science is concerned with describing and explaining how things *are*; not with prescribing how things *should be*. Therefore, science does not address

questions of *value*—whether one way is better than another (Babbie, 1986, p. 17). Scientists do not attempt to advise or recommend solutions to problems; only to understand them.

3. Social science aims **to predict and to explain**. Some scientific research seeks to *describe or predict* relationships among variables that occur in the natural world. Called *correlational research*, this type of inquiry looks for associations, or the co-occurrence of one variable with another. Associations allow scientists to make predictions that certain variables will occur together, but associations do not account for why the relationship between variables exists. Other scientific research seeks to explain, or find causes for, phenomena. Called *explanatory research*, this form of inquiry looks for causal relationships among variables. To identify causes, researchers must conduct experiments, which test causal relationships by manipulating variables under controlled conditions, and observing the results. Experiments are the only way to determine causality, since they are designed to eliminate all alternative explanations for research findings.

4. Social science often involves **reasoning with statistics**. Statistics are mathematical tools that aid in gaining knowledge from scientific research. In *quantitative research*, statistics are applied to observations, which are translated into numerical data. Statistics are used to summarize these data and to draw inferences about the overall conclusions which can reasonably be drawn from the data (Williams, 1986). More specifically, when scientists test theoretical hypotheses using a sample of individuals representing a certain population, statistics are used to help them decide whether their predicted relationship has a high probability of existing in the overall population. Without statistics, scientists would have no means for generalizing their results beyond just the sample that they observed.

Activities of Social Science

To come up with predictions and explanations, social scientists develop theories, or logical explanations about the way things occur in the world. Theories involve the rational process of identifying logical relationships among the factors contributing to a phenomenon. Social scientists then test their theories by doing empirical research (systematic observation) to find whether those logical relationships actually exist in the real world. So research, or observation, provides the means for testing theory (Babbie, 1986, p. 16).

Deduction and Induction in the Process of Scientific Inquiry

Scientific scholars go through a 3-step process as they seek to create knowledge. They ask questions, they observe, and they construct answers, or theories. Most scientists first construct theories, then test their theoretical hypotheses through observation (called the *deductive* method). However, the steps in the process of scientific inquiry are not necessarily linear or one-directional. In actual research, these steps are interrelated. Observations may suggest new questions, which may lead to modifications in theory (called the *inductive* method). Social scientific theory and research are therefore connected through two logical methods: deduction (reasoning from the whole to its parts), in which theories generate hypotheses about observations, and induction (reasoning from parts to the whole), in which specific observations generate hypotheses and theories. In this way, social science is a dynamic process in which induction alternates with deduction (Babbie, 1986, p. 46).

The Importance of Theory

Let's examine why theories are so important in social science. Theories are scholars' systematic explanations for observed facts that relate to a particular aspect of social life—in our case, communication. In an important way, theories are maps of reality (Griffin, 1997, p. 4). They help us understand why people act the way they do, and they enable us to predict and influence future events. They also draw our attention to important facets of everyday life. They help us decide what is important and what is not important in explaining human behavior. They are pieces of the puzzle of social life. Good social science theories accurately describe or explain important social phenomena with relative simplicity. Social scientists test their theories, and attempt to gather support for general principles that apply across many individuals and conditions. By testing theories, researchers gain knowledge, and humankind progresses in understanding. Social scientists pool their findings to build a collective body of knowledge about how human beings operate in the world.

Theory Building and Theory Testing

Theory building and theory testing are the basic activities of the social scientist. How do social scientists build and test their theories? Without going into detail here, we can briefly summarize the activities in the traditional scientific method. Very simply, there are five general steps (Babbie, 1986, pp. 58-59).

1. Constructing the theory: a social scientist develops a theory to describe or explain an aspect of human behavior. Theory construction is a careful, rigorous process of logically depicting how designated concepts relate to each other and thereby explain how some aspect of human social life works, based on existing knowledge.

2. Formulating theoretical hypotheses. From this theory, the social scientist derives hypotheses, or specific, measurable predictions, about how the concepts comprising the theory relate to each other.

3. Operationalizing concepts. Since theoretical concepts are abstract and somewhat vague, the social scientist must identify

precise, specific, empirical (observable) indicators, or variables, which enable her to measure the concept.

4. <u>Collecting empirical data</u>: the researcher then collects empirical data on the variables representing theoretical concepts. She might collect data from the natural world to identify associations between variables, or she might conduct experimental research to determine causal relationships.

5. <u>Empirical testing of hypotheses</u>. The last step is to statistically test the theoretical hypothesis to determine whether it is supported by the data. If the study is well designed and the statistical test shows a significant association between factors, or a significant difference between experimental groups, we can be about 95% sure that the study results were due to the hypothesized (predicted) relationship, and not to chance. If the hypothesis test shows no statistical significance, then the hypothesis is not supported by the data in this study, and the researcher would carefully reconsider her methods, her hypothesis, and ultimately her theory.

The Challenges Facing Social Science

Social science faces difficulties that the physical sciences do not. It has a reputation of being a "soft science" because of its imprecise nature. Relative to the "hard" sciences such as physics and chemistry, which measure objects and events that do not have much individual variation, social science is considerably "messier." Why? First, studying human behavior is complex, since humans are individuals who think and act based on multiple factors. Humans behave with a great deal of variability, and may not act in conclusively predictable ways. Because of human variation, researchers need to observe a sample of people that is large enough to be assured that their experimental results are not just due to chance. For results to apply beyond just the individuals in the sample, researchers also need to make sure that their sample is representative of the larger population of people from which it is taken.

Another reason why social science is naturally imprecise is that the phenomena social scientists study are abstract; they are not concrete and easily measurable. Measurements of abstract concepts depend on observable, measurable indicators, which are never completely accurate or precise. So the best that social scientists can do is use approximate indicators of theoretical concepts to discover partial (incomplete) predictions or explanations for human behavior. Because of these limitations, social science research is a never-ending effort in which researchers continually examine their results in order to gain a more accurate understanding of social phenomena (Babbie, 1986, p. 60).

Summary: The Nature of Social Science

Social science assumes there is one, universal truth about human experience that can be discovered by using the scientific method to make observations in the natural world. Scientific inquiry is designed to protect against the mistakes people tend to make in their informal questioning of why things are the way they are. Social science is objective, descriptive, and it aims to predict or explain human behavior. Statistics are used in quantitative social research to make inferences about an overall population that can be concluded from observed results in a sample of people. Social science involves theory building and theory testing, and uses both deduction and induction. Theories are logical explanations for social phenomena, and by testing theories, social scientists add to the collective body of knowledge. The scientific method consists of constructing a theory, formulating hypotheses, operationalizing concepts, collecting empirical data, and empirically testing hypotheses. Social science faces challenges that the physical sciences do not, because of its imprecise, abstract nature.

With this basic understanding of social science in mind, we can now describe how communication came to be studied by social scientists.

Emergence of Social Science in the Late 19th Century

The roots of social science lie in the discipline of psychology, the study of mental processes and behavior. Social scientific psychology evolved from the work of Wilhelm Wundt in the 1880's at the University of Leipzig, in Germany. Wundt believed that human behavior was governed, like everything else in nature, by natural laws, and that these laws could be discovered by applying the experimental methods used in the natural sciences. His methods were crude by today's standards. For example, in his institute, Wundt and his students played the roles of both experimenter and subject. The number of subjects in his experiments was small; sometimes only one, and subjects' names were usually published. Experimental psychology was dominated by German researchers until the late 1800's, but the center of the study of psychology moved to America after the outbreak of World War I, in 1917. American psychological research differed from Wundt's model in that subjects were anonymous and unknown to the researcher, and the number of subjects in an experiment was large (Rogers, 1997, p. 164-166).

The social science approach to communication study in America was shaped by the ideas of three famous European social theorists of the 1800's. The Englishman Charles Darwin's theory of evolution prompted the study of nonverbal communication in humans, and influenced the sociologists of the Chicago School, who viewed communication as a process of symbolic interaction. In Germany, Karl Marx was influenced by evolutionary theory, and his theory of dialectical materialism, in conjunction with Freudian theory, has influenced the critical school of communication, also known as the Frankfurt School and the Institute for Social Research. Austrian Sigmund Freud's psychoanalytic theory explained human behavior by examining the individual's unconscious mind. Although Freud used in-depth case studies (not scientific methods) to develop his theory, his ideas influenced Clark Hull's learning theory, which in turn influenced Carl Hovland's persuasion research. Freud's psychoanalytic theory also influenced political scientist Harold Lasswell. The interactional school of communication (Watslavick, Beavin & Jackson, 1967), which examines human behavior as a function of interpersonal communication, was a reaction to Freud's intrapersonal view that behavior results from individual forces (Rogers, 1994, pp. 33-125).

Darwin, Marx, and Freud revolutionized 19th century ideas about human behavior and society. Their work had great impact on the early social sciences in America, and on the scientific study of communication. Their ideas are still evident in some contemporary theories of communication.

Early Efforts at Scientific Study of Communication: 1920's to 1940's

Social science as we now know it took shape largely at the University of Chicago during the 1920's and 1930's. Researchers in sociology and other social science disciplines explored all parts of their environment that would help them understand society. Attempting to emulate the research practices of the physical and biological sciences, these researchers were committed to using empirical research methods to "quantify" their findings. There was a flurry of activity formulating hypotheses, gathering data, and conducting experiments to test their theories (Schramm, 1997). Among the early social science researchers in the United States was Charles Woolbert. His theory of persuasion was published in the Quarterly Journal of Speech in 1919, and his 1920 study of the effects of differing modes of public speaking may have been the first truly experimental communication study published in the U.S. (Becker, 1989).

World War II had a tremendous impact on the study of communication. It brought together, in Washington, D.C., four social scientists from different fields who are now considered the forerunners of the scientific study of communication (Rogers, 1994; Schramm, 1997): political scientist Harold Lasswell, sociologist Paul Lazarsfeld, social psychologist Kurt Lewin, and experimental psychologist Carl Hovland. Each of these men helped launch the scientific study of communication by conducting wartime research. The U.S. military considered communication vital in wartime efforts to influence the public and to train servicemen. The War Department needed to find effective ways to inform the American public about our goals in the war and about the need for food and gas rationing, and to motivate the public to support the war effort by growing victory gardens, and purchasing war bonds. In addition, the Department of the Army needed to find ways to efficiently and effectively train personnel for military service (Rogers, 1997, pp. 10-12).

All four of these trailblazers who first studied communication were brilliant, highly educated men with interdisciplinary interests, and who interacted with other great minds. Like the ancient sophists, each began to study communication when he confronted "real world" problems. Each of them profoundly influenced young scholars who later excelled in their own intellectual work (Schramm, 1997). Brief descriptions of the work of these four pioneers will help us gain a historical and biographical perspective on the development of the scientific study of communication. We begin with political scientist Harold Lasswell.

Harold Lasswell

Lasswell was a young political science scholar during the 1920's in Chicago. During his studies he met and was influenced by great thinkers of his day, including the philosophers George Herbert Mead, John Dewey, and Alfred North Whitehead. He published his dissertation, a classic analysis of World War I propaganda, in 1927. Almost all the empirical research Lasswell did involved the study of symbols. He helped launch the journal, *Public Opinion Quarterly* in 1937. He spent from 1926 to 1938 as an instructor at the University of Chicago. After 1938, he wrote and lectured. And like many other academics of that time, when World War II started he went to work as an expert for the government, directing a research project analyzing the content of world revolutionary propaganda at the U.S. Library of Congress. Some major recurring themes in his writings were power, propaganda, public opinion, and the future. Lasswell's famous communication model, "who says what in which channel to whom with what effect?" (Lasswell, 1948) provided the unifying framework for much of the U.S. wartime research, and for later communication research (Schramm, 1997, pp. 26-31).

Although Lasswell was trained as a political scientist, he was interdisciplinary in his scholarship, incorporating ideas from sociology, psychology, and philosophy. Lasswell contributed to the field of communication in three important ways. First, he encouraged the development of the communication research method of content analysis. He deeply appreciated the complexity of social data and social life, so he was reluctant to rely on quantitative analysis, and always sought to Aget behind the data" (Schramm, 1997, p. 34). Second, Lasswell gave us a comprehensive understanding of propaganda--the control of opinions, through suggestion and illusion, by significant symbols such as stories, rumors, reports, and pictures. He believed propaganda was so important because it was a symbolic alternative to coercion and violence. Third, Lasswell conceptualized the political role of communication as encompassing multiple important functions in society, including informing, responding to information, and socializing citizens (Schramm, 1997, pp. 38-39).

Paul Lazarsfeld

Paul Lazarsfeld was born in Vienna in 1901. He received his doctorate in mathematics, and soon founded a research institute in Vienna which conducted commercial research on a variety of social and psychological topics. His chief tool was the survey, and his early work was the precursor to market research. During the depression, Lazarsfeld moved to America to flee Hitler's regime. Here he established another research institute which later became the Office of Radio Research at Columbia University. In the 1930's, radio was relatively new, and potentially as influential as TV was in the 1950's. The Office of Radio Research studied media audiences, and the sociologist Lazarsfeld believed he could study audiences to learn the reasons why they listen to radio and see films. Lazarsfeld concluded that the mass media met important needs for people, that mass media influenced the public indirectly, and the influence of media was socially reinforcing, but not dangerous. Lazarsfeld became a professor of sociology at Columbia, and the radio research project there eventually became the Bureau of Applied Social Research. It was the only research organization of its kind, and was of vital importance both to the development of mass media and to the academic study of mass communication. Lazarsfeld's great contribution to the field of communication study was his creativity—the creative ways in which he conducted field research and brought researchers together to work on problems (Schramm, 1997, pp. 45-63). Of the 4 pioneers, Lazarsfeld was most interested in mass communication and its effects.

Kurt Lewin

Kurt Lewin (1890-1947) is considered one of the founders of experimental social psychology. Like Paul Lazarsfeld, he fled to

America from Hitler's regime. Originally a Gestalt psychologist, Lewin conducted classic experiments in group communication. He is known for his research and training in group dynamics, and for developing the participative management style in organizations. Lewin's field theory described the forces in an individual's social environment, including small groups, that influence individual behavior. Lewin was committed to applied research. His major studies dealt with social problems such as prejudice, and authoritarian leadership. He was a "practical theorist" who believed in testing theories by applying them to social problems in real life (Rogers, 1994, pp. 354-355). It was Kurt Lewin who stated, "there's nothing as practical as a good theory." Lewin was a mentor for many famous social psychologists, including Leon Festinger, Harold Kelley, and Stanley Schachter.

Lewin combined a humanistic and scientific approach to studying human behavior. He was interested in individual subjective experiences as well as group similarities. He avoided using statistical tests of significance because he was concerned that the individual case would be lost in the aggregation of data involved in statistical analysis (Rogers, 1994, p. 321). Lewin was the first to emphasize the cognitive approach in social psychology—the idea that an individual's thoughts both produce, and are the product of, communication. Lewinian research on the effects of groups on individuals continued through the 1950's, but in the 1960's, interest in social psychology shifted away from group influences to the study of more intrapersonal cognitive explanations for individual behavior. Today, there is little research going on in the area of group dynamics, but traces of Lewin's thinking still linger in communication research (Rogers, 1994, pp. 320-355).

Carl Hovland

Carl Hovland was an experimental psychologist who studied the effects of persuasion in the 1940's and 50's. His experimental work helped inform later research in the subdisciplines of inter-personal communication and mass communication. Hovland had studied under Clark Hull, the behaviorist who developed learning theory based on the ideas of classical conditioning and Freudian psychoanalysis.

In 1942, at age 30, Hovland left Yale University to direct a research program for the U.S. Department of War. He headed the experimental unit in the Research Branch, and worked alongside several up-and-coming Yale psychologists like Irving Janis, plus consultants such as Paul Lazarsfeld and Rensis Likert (Rogers, 1994, p. 362). Hovland's primary focus was investigating the factors involved in attitude change. The Army needed to train 15 million new soldiers to fight in World War II, and Hovland's research unit studied the effects of training films on soldiers. The researchers examined the effects of one-sided and two-sided persuasive messages, source credibility, and fear appeals on knowledge and attitudes of soldiers. Hovland analyzed how individuals learn from communication messages, and developed the "message-learning approach" to attitude change. He used the components of Shannon's linear model of communication—source, message, channel, and receiver, as independent variables in his experiments. A brilliant thinker, he designed ingenious experiments to test the effects of each of these variables on attitude change. He later returned to Yale, and continued this research in an extensive series of studies under the Yale communication research program. The accumulated work of the Yale program produced a comprehensive understanding of persuasion, and is considered by many as "the largest single contribution to communication any man has made" (Rogers, 1994, p. 366-381).

Hovland and his group of researchers wrote almost a book a year on persuasion from 1949 until he died in 1961. Research on persuasion, which we now call social influence, continued, and was especially active during the 1950's and 60's. While Hovland's technique of studying persuasion as one-way messages is now considered an oversimplification of the interactive nature of communication, his work is considered seminal by social influence scholars (Rogers, 1994, p. 384-385).

Looking back at the early work of Lasswell, Lazarsfeld, Lewin and Hovland, it is clear that the emergence of mass media and social concerns in America from the 1930's to 1950's stimulated the growth of communication study by social scientists. Mass media, war, and rapid technological change profoundly affected all human communication, and presented society with unprecedented problems and opportunities ripe for social research. Lasswell was concerned with propaganda, and Lazarsfeld was interested in the effects of the mass media on audiences. Lewin investigated the effects of social environments and group dynamics, and Hovland studied how mass media could be used persuasively. All four men applied their research to compelling social problems.

We can see from these biographical sketches that while scholars in speech departments focused their attention primarily on speeches and speech making, the broader study of communication attracted scholars from other social science disciplines—sociology, political science, experimental psychology, gestalt psychology, even anthropology. The social scientific study of communication was occurring in response to social needs and technological change, but it was scattered across disparate disciplines with different intellectual roots. The first scholar to appreciate the range of researchers who shared a common interest in exploring the process and function of communication was Wilbur Schramm. Schramm took an interdisciplinary perspective and sought to bring together scholars who focused on explaining human communication. To designate this interdisciplinary field of academic work, he coined the term "communication study."

Wilbur Schramm

Wilbur Schramm (1907-1987) was, in Robert Gunderson's terms, the quintessential refugee in the study of communication. Educated in the humanities, he received his Ph.D. in English literature in 1932. His dissertation was an analysis of Longfellow's epic poem, "Hiawatha." Interestingly, it was a speech defect that led to Schramm's curiosity in studying communication. He had developed a stutter as a child, and because of this problem, he avoided speaking in public, and sought help from the research in speech communication. Schramm was a brilliant thinker, a prolific writer, and a part-time journalist (Rogers, 1994, pp. 447-456).

Schramm was influenced by Lazarsfeld's and Hovland's research during and after WWII. He volunteered to work as education director of the Office of War Information, which was responsible for domestic and foreign propaganda. There, he designed public information campaigns and studied their effects by using audience surveys. He helped draft speeches for Franklin Roosevelt's radio broadcasts, including his fireside chats (Rogers, 1994, pp. 12-23).

In 1943, at the University of Iowa, Schramm organized the first Ph.D. interdisciplinary program in communication study in the School of Journalism. Schramm's program was not the only program at the University of Iowa offering a degree in communication. The Department of Speech and Dramatic Arts, Charles Woolbert's home department, was the first academic department in the United States to study speech scientifically. Their work pioneered the study of interpersonal communication, and their students were awarded degrees in communication.

Since Schramm's Ph.D. was in the humanities, he was not acceptable as a faculty member of social science departments such as sociology or psychology, but he and his innovative program were accepted in the Department of Journalism. The doctoral program curriculum in mass communication included courses in psychology, sociology, and political science. In 1947 Schramm moved to the University of Illinois, and became Dean of the Division of Communication, which included the School of Journalism, the university's radio and TV stations, and publicity offices for university alumni, athletics, and agriculture among others. He became known there as the "communication czar." To improve the scientific credibility of his students, Schramm founded research institutes at the University of Iowa, the University of Illinois, and later at Stanford University. These research institutes were more flexible than university departments. They offered valuable apprentice-style training for doctoral students, and facilitated collaboration with other social science disciplines (Rogers, 1994, p. 24-29).

Identifying himself as a communication scholar, Schramm organized academic programs to study communication at three major universities; trained the first generation communication social scientists; and wrote groundbreaking textbooks for communication courses. He was the first person to hold the title "professor of communication." Schramm's prolific writings helped shape the field of communication from 1948 through 1977 (Rogers, 1994, pp. 29, 446-447). His vision was an integrated social science of human communication. Existing departments of speech and journalism would be merged into one department that would treat communication generically, and could include study of interpersonal communication and media technologies. These new areas would be added to (or replace) the traditional, skills-centered speech and journalism curricula (Schramm, 1997, pp. 156-157).

Schramm's vision and work fundamentally altered the field of communication study. During the 1960s, 70s and 80s, his approach was widely adopted in American colleges and universities. Its adoption took three forms:

1. Some universities, often with the support of major private grant funding, formed schools or divisions of communication. These

include the Annenberg Schools of Communication at the University of Southern California, and Pennsylvania State University, the School of Communication at the University of Texas, and the School of Mass Communication at Stanford.

2. Some speech departments eliminated or sharply curtailed their research and instruction in the skill-oriented study of public speaking, and shifted their emphasis almost entirely to focus on interpersonal and mass communication. These departments turned away from rhetorical scholarship in favor of an exclusively social scientific approach. The primary example of this approach is Michigan State University, where major contributions were made in communication research and theory under the leadership of David Berlo and, later, Gerald Miller. Other important examples are the University of West Virginia and the University of Arizona.

3. The most common manner in which Schramm's integrated view of communication was adopted was assimilation into existing departments of speech. Recognizing that significant new knowledge about communication could be developed using social science methods, and with an interdisciplinary perspective, speech and rhetoric scholars expanded their research efforts, their methods, and their course curricula. Seeking a useful marriage of rhetorical and social scientific scholarship, many changed their department names to "speech communication." During the 1960's and 70's, they added courses in interpersonal communication and mass communication. Major Midwestern universities, such as Wisconsin, Minnesota, and Indiana exemplified this approach.

This common approach, involving a blending of rhetorical and social science scholarship, was also reflected in the development of our professional associations. The major organization for teachers and scholars of rhetoric began in 1914, and soon changed its name to the Speech Association of America (SAA), then to the

Speech Communication Association (SCA) in 1969, and recently to the National Communication Association (NCA). The National Society for the Study of Communication, later known as the International Communication Association (ICA) was established in 1950 by communication scholars who believed the SAA was not adequately concerned with communication problems in business and industry, or with social scientific approaches to studying communication. Today, NCA tends to emphasize historical and critical approaches, and the majority of its large membership identifies with the speech and rhetoric orientation to the discipline. In contrast, ICA focuses more on social scientific approaches, and provides an intellectual home for scientific researchers in communication. However there is a large overlap in the membership and the subject areas of these two organizations (Becker, 1989; Pearce, 1985).

The Growth of Social Science in Communication Study

Classical rhetorical theory articulated a clear set of discrete communication variables for social scientists to investigate. Early social science studies often focused on testing these variables. Aristotle's ideas on the use of fear appeals and the role of ethos in persuasion are evident in a large portion of the work of Hovland's communication research program at Yale (Hovland, Janis & Kelly, 1953). Hovland's empirical approach to persuasion was even called "scientific rhetoric." (Maccoby, 1963). Later, Aristotle's dimensions of ethos (source credibility) were refined by the scientific work of David Berlo and James McCroskey (Becker, 1989). For the most part, these studies confirmed Aristotle's 2500-year old observations. It was almost immediately evident, however, that scientific research would have to move beyond classical rhetoric, and draw upon social science theories to build the understanding of human communication that was needed in the twentieth century.

In the 1950's, doctoral programs and related research centers for the study of communication began to appear. It was becoming increasingly clear that many of the important problems of this time were communication problems, and that studying these problems required insights and methods from several disciplines (Schramm, 1989, p. 19). Courses in communication theory drew on theories from all the behavioral sciences, and the staffs of research institutes included sociologists, psychologists, anthropologists and political scientists. The research methods used included experimentation, survey research, and content analysis.

After WWII, when many state universities became research universities, departments were expected to produce research, as well as instruction. In the 1950's social scientists adopted the term "communication research," and helped build the International Communication Association. Communication scholarship moved toward empirical, quantitative, research that was focused on effects of communication. About this time Shannon & Weaver developed their linear model of communication, and the scientific approach began to have a strong impact on the field (Griffin, 1997, p. 23).

Although public speaking remained the most widely enrolled course offered by communication departments, by 1970, interpersonal communication had become the central focus for communication scholars. The encounter group movement influenced many instructors, and emphasis on persuasion was reduced. In the 1970's, important new interpersonal communication theories like Berger's Uncertainty Reduction theory and McCroskey's model of communication apprehension began to appear. These theories marked the beginning of a rapid expansion in interpersonal communication theory.

In the 1980's & 1990's, social scientific communication theories have greatly increased. Communication departments are growing in size and number, and several divergent trends in communication scholarship and research are emerging. Two major trends in graduate level scholarship are occurring: one is toward empirical, quantitative perspectives and methods; the other is toward postmodern critical studies of rhetoric and culture (Rogers, 1994, p. 491). Trends in social scientific research include an emphasis on mental structures and cognitive processes in communication, continued focus on interpersonal relationships; and practical application of theories of mass communication and social influence to social and behavioral problems. There is also growing interest in postmodern research, especially cultural studies and feminist criticism, and in more ethnographic research. In short, communication research and theory today have become more specialized, fragmented, and multi-focused; drawing from both social science and rhetorical methods of inquiry. The social science and rhetorically-based approaches represent very different scholarly perspectives, yet they both occupy an important place within the discipline (Griffin, 1997, pp. 28-30).

By the 1990's, an estimated 1,500 schools or departments of communication existed at US universities and colleges. The major growth spurt occurred during the 60's, but steady growth has continued since then. Undergraduate enrollment increased dramatically during the 70's and 80's. The applied aspect of communication study is very popular among students, partly because it leads to jobs after graduation. Today the field of communication has both an applied orientation (at the undergraduate level) and a theoretical/research orientation at the graduate level. Communication continues to be a professional field as well as an academic discipline (Rogers, 1994, p. 479-481).

Summary

While the discipline of speech was dominated by Neo-Aristotelian rhetorical scholars, it was primarily scholars in related disciplines who made good on Woolbert's claims, developing of the social science of communication study. As a result of their work the scope of communication study was broadened to include the full range of human communication activity. Sometimes building on classical rhetorical concepts, and sometimes developing theories from other roots, social science communication scholars redefined the entire study of human communication. Joined by speech communication scholars who adopted their view of the discipline, they have persistently refined and improved their research methods. Their work has contributed a significant body of both theoretical and practical knowledge to our maturing discipline.

References

Babbie, E. (1986). *The practice of social research*. Belmont, CA: Wadsworth Publishing Co.

Becker, S. L. (1989). The rhetorical tradition. In S. S. King (Ed.), *Human communication as a field of study* (pp. 27-41). Albany, NY: State University of New York Press.

Griffin, E. (1997). *A first look at communication theory*. New York: McGraw-Hill.

Hovland, C. I., Janis, I. L., & Kelley, H. H. (1953). *Communication and persuasion*. New Haven, CT: Yale University Press.

King, S. S. (1989). Communication: Roots, visions, and prospects. In S. S. King (Ed.), *Human communication as a field of study* (pp. 1-11). Albany, NY: State University of New York Press.

Lasswell, H. (1948). The structure and function of communication in society. In L. Bryson (Ed.), *The communication of ideas* (pp. 37-51). New York: Institute for Religious Studies.

Pearce, W. B. (1985). Scientific methods in communication studies and their implications for theory and research. In T. W. Benson (Ed.), *Speech communication in the 20th century* (pp. 255-281). Carbondale and Edwardsville, IL: Southern Illinois University Press.

Maccoby. (1963). The new "scientific" rhetoric. In W. Schramm (Ed.), *The science of human communication: New directions and new findings in communication research*. New York: Basic Books.

Rogers, E. M. (1994). *A history of communication study: A biographical approach*. New York: The Free Press.

Schramm, W. (1989). Human communication as a field of behavioral science: Jack Hilgard and his committee. In S. S. King (Ed.), *Human communication as a field of study* (pp. 13-26). Albany, NY: State University of New York Press.

Schramm, W. (1997). (S.H. Chaffee & E. M. Rogers, Eds.) *The beginnings of communication study in America: A personal memoir*. Thousand Oaks, CA: Sage.

Watzlavick, P., Beavin, J., & Jackson, D.D. (1967). *Pragmatics of human communication: A study of interactional patterns, pathologies, and paradoxes*. New York: W. W. Norton & Co.

Williams, F. (1986). *Reasoning with statistics*. New York: Holt, Rinehart and Winston.

Chapter 5
Enduring Issues and Enduring Value: Communication Study Today

When we look at the long history of communication study, and reflect on our own careers as communication scholars and practitioners, three broad conclusions seem obvious: (1) Our heritage as a discipline lies in both the rhetorical tradition and the social science approach. (2) Communication scholars and practitioners will continue to struggle with fundamental issues concerning the nature, purpose, and merit of their work. And, (3) the systematic study of communication will continue because it has great value. In this closing chapter, we briefly discuss the enduring issues and the enduring value of the study of human communication.

Enduring Issues

There are four sets of fundamental issues concerning the study of human communication with which communication scholars and teachers have struggled since Plato's time. These issue sets center around the following questions:

1. What is communication? And what is the proper scope of communication study?

2.   What are the primary purposes of communication study?
3.   What methods are most appropriate for studying communication?
4.   What is the value of communication study? How does communication study relate to the pursuit of truth? What about the dark side of communication? In other words, where do we stand in our struggle with Plato's Shadow?

Each of these questions is discussed below.

The Nature of Communication and the Scope of Communication Study

Long ago, Aristotle defined "rhetoric" as the "art of discovering all the available means of persuasion in a given situation." For him, communication was all about persuasion. Communication was a conscious, strategic, purposive activity. Plato, on the other hand, preferred to view communication as a cooperative inquiry in pursuit of Truth. For Plato, communication was a purposive, strategic activity on the part of the teacher, though perhaps not for the student. Since Aristotle's and Plato's time, every serious thinker about communication has struggled with the question of how best to define this subject. Twentieth century communication scholars continue to wrestle with important issues of definition. Contemporary issues of definition revolve around such questions as:

*   Does communication have to occur between two or more persons in order to be considered communication? Or, does should talking to myself (intrapersonal communication) be considered communication?
*   Does communication have to involve people at all to be considered communication? Should interaction with other animals or between other animals be included in the study of communication?

- Does the intention of the communicator matter in determining whether to consider a behavior communication? Has communication occurred if a "receiver" believes s/he has received a message, even though the supposed sender of the message did not intend to communicate?
- Does our subject include the *content* of messages, or are we concerned exclusively with the *process* of communication? In other words, is it the message sent that should be considered communication? Or, is it the interaction of the sender and receiver of the message?
- Is there such a thing as a *communication episode*? Or, is communication an on-going system of multiple interactions, with no identifiable boundaries?
- Where, if at all, should we place the boundaries that mark where the study of communication stops, and some other discipline begins?

All of these questions remain open to varying answers. Fundamental questions about how we should define the term "communication" have been present in our study for 2500 years. Issues of definition and scope have multiplied in the 20th century, as our knowledge of the subject and of research methods has increased. We see no indication that an overarching consensus definition will develop in the foreseeable future. Yet, there has been progress toward agreement on elements of a definition. Communication scholars today generally agree that communication is an ongoing transactional process in which both senders and receivers of messages play active roles. Greater agreement about the definition and scope of communication study may help solidify our status as a discipline.

The Primary Purposes of Communication Study

Throughout the social sciences, issues of purpose divide scholars into competing camps. Some insist that the scholar's purpose is to conduct "pure" research, generating new theory and knowledge. Their purpose is pure pursuit of truth; as social scientists, they seek to *describe* rather than to *prescribe*. For other scholars, the purpose of research is practical application; they seek to find and *prescribe* solutions to identified problems through their scholarly work. This "pure research" versus "applied research" controversy is especially intense in the discipline of communication, where it mixes with old the problem of Plato's Shadow. Remember that it was the *practical problem* of individuals needing to develop skill in persuasion for political and economic gain to which the sophists responded by inventing the study of communication. It was the *practical art* of rhetoric that Plato decried in the *Gorgias*. In his later work, the *Phaedrus,* Plato continued to minimize the value of studying rhetoric, but he allowed that something like a pure "science" which sought to understand the essential nature of human communication might be worth a philosopher's effort. Plato was absolutely correct in pointing out that rhetoric could be used to hide the truth as well as to present the truth.

Teachers of public speaking, focused as they are on helping students with the practical problem of presenting themselves and their subjects well rather than on discovering any new and universal truths, tend to be viewed as contemporary sophists in an academic world so influenced by Plato. So are consultants, who dispense communication advice to clients. Public relations specialists and press secretaries are seen as a bit glamorous on one hand, but ethically suspect on the other. And marketing and advertising are seen as economically productive, but morally doubtful. Clearly, applied research, and practical application of communication research, can involve the dark side of communication, and certainly both require laboring in Plato's Shadow. On the other hand, it is the need for practical skills that draws students to communication courses. And, it is the need for practical solutions to social problems that generates grant funding for communication research.

This problem may be exacerbated by the advocates of pure research in communication, who tend to be firmly committed to social scientific principles. These pure researchers may be especially harsh in criticizing application-oriented scholars, because they sense the need to dispel Plato's Shadow from their own work.

Appropriate Methods in Communication Study

Among communication scholars, debates about issues of definition, scope, and purpose are intertwined with issues of method. At the core of these debates are philosophical questions about the nature of truth, and the nature of reality; and epistemological disputes about the nature of knowledge. Traditional social scientists assume a logical positivist stance philosophically. They assume that one true reality exists; that reality is knowable only through sensory data; and that certain knowledge can be achieved only through scientific methods. Therefore, traditional social scientists tend to disparage the methods of rhetorical and social critics. They view postmodern methods as a corruption of genuine scholarship.

Postmodern theorists and critics begin with a fundamentally different philosophical stance. They assume that, while physical nature may exist as a single reality that is knowable through science, human cultures and societies are made up of social realities. Social realities, they insist, are not the same as the "hard reality" of physical nature, and cannot be understood or evaluated by applying methods borrowed from the physical sciences. There are many different social realities, each created and sustained by people through communication. Postmodernists argue that contemporary science, and the institutions and intellectual conventions that support it, are themselves social realities. Postmodern critics seek to evaluate the various social reality systems, to expose the ethical flaws in such systems, and to propose ways to improve them. The philosophical stance of postmodern scholars leads them to address fundamentally different questions than do social scientists, and to adopt correspondingly different methods.

Social scientists and postmodern critics both tend to treat the applied, practical art of rhetoric as useful, but of lesser value than scholarly research. They are comfortable with Plato's comparison of the practical art of rhetoric with "cookery." Perhaps even more than the general public, they tend to be suspicious of communication practitioners, such as advertisers and public relations specialists, doubting their motives and their interest in discovering truth. Both groups of scholars tend to place the teacher of public speaking at the bottom of the status ladder among communication professionals.

We understand the deep philosophical differences that drive the controversy over methods among communication scholars. But we think it is unnecessary and unfortunate. Both rhetorical and social science perspectives are useful, and both can gain from each other. Postmodern rhetorical criticism is humanistic in its purposes and methods. C. Arthur VanLear suggests that humanistic and scientific scholarship engage one another in a dialectical relationship in which each contributes to the advance of the other (personal communication, April 11, 1998). Stephen Littlejohn points out that "Almost any program of research and theory building includes some aspects of both scientific and humanistic scholarship." "At times," he says, "the scientist is a humanist, using intuition, creativity, interpretation, and insight... In turn, at times the humanist must be scientific, seeking facts that enable experience to be understood" (Littlejohn, 1999, 11). Marie

Hochmuth Nichols, the distinguished rhetorician, stated that the "humanities without science are blind, but science without the humanities may be vicious" (Nichols, 1963, p. 18).

We agree that studying human communication requires both scientific and humanistic methods, and that scientists and humanists depend upon one another. In any specific study, the choice of methods must depend on the research questions addressed, and the nature of available data. Moreover, we note that the study of human communication was born as an applied art, in response to practical needs. Our wish is to see the advocates of competing approaches in communication study begin to focus on ways their scholarship can be mutually supportive, how it can better inform communication practitioners, and how it can be applied to improve communication problems in the world.

Our Struggle with Plato's Shadow

The dark side of communication study, that is, the potential for communication knowledge and skill to be used in the service of promoting falsehood, is clearly more present and potent than ever. The more we know about how people process information, and how they are influenced by persuasive efforts, the more possible it is for unethical persons to mislead and control others. Today we live in an electronically mediated world where news is constantly managed and influenced by "spin masters." We are exposed to constant, highly sophisticated advertising. As a matter of self-defense, citizens must become genuinely cynical about messages, about practitioners who create messages, and about the theorists who inform those practitioners. "Sophistry," in the most pejorative sense of the term, abounds.

On the other hand, Aristotle's rationale for proceeding with the study and teaching of rhetoric seems more relevant today than ever. If ethical people fail to learn and skillfully use the best available

communication principles and tools, unethical, self-serving manipu-
lators will have their way, and control our minds, spirits, and material
goods. Carl Hovland and his colleagues exemplified Aristotle's
rationale when they developed persuasion theory for the purpose
of countering Hitler's propaganda in World War II. Contemporary
health communication researchers exemplify this rationale when
they employ persuasion theories to develop and test mass media
anti-smoking campaigns, which counter the pervasive advertising
of cigarette companies. Communication skills, communication
technology, and communication theories are powerful tools. It is
imperative today that good people master and use them.

Why, then, are communication scholars, teachers, and practitioners still doing battle with Plato's Shadow? It may be that Plato's
pejorative characterization of the sophists and their work is so
deeply rooted in Western Culture that the shadow is permanent.
Our academic culture, with its powerful commitment to pure research—to the acquisition of knowledge for the sake of
knowledge—tends to devalue matters of practical application. The
ideology of modern science, which values development and testing of theories above all else, tends to diminish any study whose
focus is practical. And the dark side of communication remains
ever present to provide credible evidence to support the disparag-
ing of communication study and practice. The shadow Plato cast
over the study of communication will likely remain present and
troublesome.

The Enduring Value of the Study of Communication

In Chapter 1, we introduced the idea of Plato's Shadow by
telling the story of Michael's argument with a fellow faculty member—a film instructor who disapproved of teaching students to
debate, and who cited Plato and Socrates to support his position.
There is a sequel to that story, and the sequel is also worth telling.

About three years after the "boxing Plato's Shadow" discussion, the department decided against granting tenure to the film instructor. The department had violated its own official procedures in making this decision to deny tenure, but the university administration concurred in the decision. The film instructor, who was married with three children to support, found himself facing unemployment. His only hope was to file and win a grievance case against the university. But grievance cases are matters of argument, and he lacked the necessary skills. Nor could he afford to hire a lawyer to advocate his case. So, he turned to Michael Dues, the debate coach, for help. Using the very rhetorical skills of which the film instructor so sternly disapproved, the debate coach advocated and won his grievance case, saving his job and his livelihood. The film instructor was grateful, but he never became comfortable with the processes of argument and debate.

Mary Brown had a comparable encounter with a colleague who was a scientific researcher for a state agency. The scientist deplored Mary's profession as a communication specialist for the agency. He considered communication practitioners "hacks," and often jokingly declared that they were a plague on society. The irony was that it was Mary's skillful communication with the state legislature that secured the funding for the very research that her colleague conducted. If it weren't for her knowledge and skills, his research could not have continued.

The point we wish to make in telling this story is that communication, including rhetorical communication, is so inherently central in human interaction that it is inescapable. Even Plato, in writing the *Gorgias,* found himself constructing arguments against rhetoric, and employing his beloved Socrates as a rhetorical device to effectively present his case. In any open and democratic society, the study and practice of human communication simply cannot be avoided. Its absolute practical value is enduring. Today the need for knowledge and skills in interpersonal, small group and organizational communication is clearer than ever. The need for skill in public speaking is clearly as great as ever. The need to develop knowledge and skills to communicate across cultures has been recognized in recent decades, and scholars are responding with research and instruction programs. The profound personal and social impacts of new communication technologies are beginning to be recognized and studied. It seems abundantly clear that the study of human communication must and will continue.

The value of maintaining a distinct academic domain of communication study also seems evident. Research pertaining to human communication will certainly continue in other disciplines. An important contribution of the discipline of communication study has been to pull together the fragments of communication knowledge developed in other disciplines into a more focused, if not a synthesized collection. Whether communication study develops as a truly distinct academic discipline or moves forward toward Schramm's vision of an interdisciplinary domain of academic endeavor, it must and will continue as an organized, professional activity.

References

Littlejohn, S. W. (1999). *Theories of Human Communication (6th ed.)*. Belmont, CA: Wadsworth Publishing Co.

Nichols, M. H. (1963). *Rhetoric and Criticism*. Baton Rouge, LA: Louisiana State University.